MW01196404

Journey of the Soul:

Finding Peace
Through Spiritual Disciplines

*A series of essays from
Christian therapists and practitioners*

Dr. Timothy Sumerlin, Editor

ISBN: 978-1-953623-86-7. Published by Illumination Publishers Intl. Printed in the United States of America.

Cover design by Roy Appalsamy of Toronto, Canada. Interior layout by Toney Mulhollan.

Our books may be purchased in bulk for promotional, educational and theological training use. Contact Illumination Publishers International at IPinfo@ipibooks.com.

About the editor: Timothy Sumerlin is a professional counselor and adjunct professor at the University of Denver. He is director of *In Motion Counseling*, and along with his wife, Jackie, created Disciples in Motion, an innovative recovery ministry helping churches all over the world. Their two children, Tim and Danielle, along with their son-in-law, Adrian, serve with a mission church in China. Tim and Jackie travel internationally, teaching churches in recovery concepts and other counseling related issues. Tim also serves as an elder in the Denver Church of Christ. For more about his ministry go to www.inmotioncounseling.org.

www.ipibooks.com

Acknowledgements

Many thanks to the editors, book designers, and cover personnel at Illumination Publishers. These passionate Christians care about getting God's heart and word out to as many as possible, and serve our fellowship tirelessly. Blessings in particular to Toney Mulhollan, Paul Vasquez, Roy Appalsamy, and Amy Morgan.

A heartfelt thanks to all the contributors of this work. What I love the most about our fellowship of churches, the ICOC, is our dedication to progress and a willingness to advance and communicate our knowledge of God as we move forward in our love for the lost and our fellow Christians around the world. Over the forty-one years I have been a part of the ICOC churches, I've seen dramatic shifts and progress in our theology, practices, and love for the Word. The spirit of restoration lives!

The men and women (therapists, ministers, counselors, teachers, and scholars) who authored these essays are often at the forefront of change in our churches. This is not always an easy place to live, but it is one that glorifies God and ultimately inspires and helps others. It is a privilege and honor to call you all friends, mentors, and companions in the faith!

Of course, all praise goes to God, our Father who loves us, Jesus his Son, whom we walk with, and the work of the Holy Spirit to inspire and guide this work! *Soli Deo Gloria!*

TABLE OF CONTENTS

TABLE OF CONTENTS

INTRODUCTION

Spiritual Disciplines
Dr. Timothy Sumerlin, PhD

Timothy Sumerlin has been a Christian for forty-one years and lives in Denver, Colorado with his wife, Jackie. They have been married thirty-seven years. They have two children (Danielle and Tim), and a brand-new granddaughter, Elsa. Timothy has worked as a counselor for over thirty years and is an adjunct professor at the University of Denver. He is the dean of the Counseling Program at the Rocky Mountain School of Ministry and Theology, as well as an elder in the Denver Church of Christ. He is also the director of In Motion Counseling, which includes Disciples In Motion, an innovative recovery program for the church setting, and The Grief Journey Program. He has authored four books: *Recovery Moving Forward: The Healings*, *The Grief Journey: Finding Peace in All of Life's Losses*, *The Recovery Journey: Jesus' Heart to Help the Hurting*, and *Journey of the Soul: Finding Peace Through Spiritual Disciplines (editor)*

Introduction

I'll never forget that day. As young marrieds and the parents of two small children, my wife, Jackie, and I were knee-deep in leadership roles in our church. We had full-time jobs (physical therapy and educator) and led a large portion of the church. Our schedules were packed from early morning to late evening most days of the week. We loved our work but were dangerously sliding into burnout.

After a Sunday afternoon leaders' meeting at our home, I walked back to our daughter's bedroom to find Jackie sitting on the floor, silent. When I inquired as to what she was doing, she replied something like, "I'm done; I can't take this anymore." Instead of sitting on the floor with her and comforting her, I (unfortunately) made a comment like, "Sure you can, let's go."

Later that year, a young Christian couple commented to our ministry leader, "We respect Tim and Jackie but would never want their lifestyle." At the time, I took this as a badge of honor. "Look at us, we're so committed." I had bought hook, line, and sinker into the "production mindset" of Christianity—that my worth was dependent on how hard I worked and what I produced. My prideful and unspiritual heart could not see the harm I was incurring on my life, on Jackie's health, on my family, and on my church.

As I look back on those years, I can now see that living like this illustrated a few schemes of Satan. Consider:

- God is after my production; that is his main concern for me.

- My worth is dependent on said production.

- My friends and neighbors saw this kind of life and often were not attracted to it.

- My faith took a hit as I witnessed many leave the faith.

- I grew envious of those who "enjoyed life" around me.

- I became resentful of the life of a disciple and wondered if I could make it to the end.

Thinking about many years of this kind of work and misunderstanding of God's desire and purpose for my life, I feel sad. How could I miss the damage we were doing?

As a Christian now of over forty years and an elder in my church, I survey the damage many of us have done to ourselves and others. I know many women who have suffered physical damage due to the kind of schedules and stress we maintained for years. People have not only left the ministry but their faith for the same reason. Families collectively lost their faith. Multitudes remain, but with caution and hesitancy to lead in any form or fashion.

And church is not the only place this occurs. Everywhere we look in our society, we see this phenomenon. Teachers, counselors, and administrators in education. Ministers, evangelists, elders, lay leaders, and members in churches. Business and financial employees. Most in the service industry suffer from long hours and lost vision for what life could be. Police officers, nurses, doctors, social workers, and therapists. And the list goes on and on.[1] Pause and consider. Look around. Listen. Is this what God made us for?

And it is not just older adults. Teenagers and young adults are experiencing the highest levels of stress, frustration, and burnout ever seen in our world. The suicide rates are at a level never seen before.[2]

Consider the following statistics on mental health in the US.[3]

- 1 in 5 US adults experience mental illness each year.
- 1 in 20 US adults experience serious mental illness each year.
- 1 in 6 US youth ages 6–17 experience a mental health disorder each year.
- 50% of all lifetime mental illness begins by age 14, and 75% by age 24. Suicide is the second leading cause of death among people ages 10–34.

While these (and other statistics) may be common knowledge, many of us are unaware of what the damaging effects are.[4] Please do your own research and see how our society, our institutions, and yes, even our churches promote an environment of extreme production and work that fosters mental health problems.

In this book you will find many practices to allow you time to slow down, quiet yourself, and find God in a new way and a new light. Is this countercultural for those of you in the ICOC? Yes, it is.

I believe our fellowship was partly built on a "production model." That is, our primary orientation is toward what we as disciples can produce for God. This can tend to be humanistic in nature and not in line with the God we see in the Scriptures. This model (in my opinion) is partially responsible for many who have not only left our fellowship over the years but have experienced damage to their faith as well. God's grace has allowed many of us to remain

---

1. https://www.apa.org/monitor/2022/01/special-burnout-stress
2. https://worldpopulationreview.com/state-rankings/suicide-rates-by-state
3. https://www.nami.org/mhstats
4. https://www.nami.org/About-Mental-Illness/Common-with-Mental-Illness/Anosognosia

in a thriving fellowship in other ways, but the model must change.

We need the continued healing hand of Jesus in our lives. Jesus practiced spiritual disciplines, and as disciples of his, we should too. Jesus kept the sabbath (Luke 4:16), meditated on the Word (Matthew 4:4), taught about the living Word (John 14:10), often withdrew to isolated places (Luke 5:16), spent time in isolated places to pray (Mark 1:35), and lived a life that avoided burnout (Luke 4:1, 10:21). He spent ample time walking, laughing, and enjoying parties and dinners, and got his rest when needed. Once he asked that no one else come into the house so he could be alone (Mark 7:24).

Many of us have spent too much time in our lives burned out and tired of the Christian walk. We don't leave our faith, because we love God and others, but we find it difficult to remain zealous and energized to serve him as we did before. Some of this may be due to simply growing older and physically not being able to maintain our previous schedules, but I think much of it is spiritual in nature. The answers often lie within.

I am grateful for the ways God has used our fellowship of churches and what we've been able to do in the church over the years in countries all over the world. I love seeing friends that are a result of our dependence on God, hard work, and faith, and watching the joy of their salvation in healed lives and families. However, I believe our orientation of work was an unhealthy one and not sustainable over the years.

Without balance and a proper orientation in trusting God to work, we can experience a fatigue that is faith damaging. We tire physically and spiritually, and our love for God may grow cold (Matthew 24:12). During my forty-one years as a Christian, I've felt this way many times in many ways. I've doubted my faith. I've had attitudes at the leaders in my church and fellowship. I've questioned God's plan for the world and for my life. At times I've grown dull to the hurts of my neighbors and my brothers and sisters in the fellowship.

I hope we all find healing in Jehovah Rapha (our God who heals). "If you listen carefully to the Lord your God and do what is right in his eyes, if you pay attention to his commands and keep all his decrees, I will not bring on you any of the diseases I brought on the Egyptians, for I am the Lord, who heals you" (Exodus 15:26).

God is an expert at healing hearts and bringing life to the dead (Ezekiel 11:19, 36:26), and this ministry of healing continues to this day with his Son, Jesus. He is the same now as he was 2000 years ago—totally invested in changing hearts and rebuilding lives. Jesus' heart was to restore us to a relationship with God, and he seems absolutely bent on doing that to his very last drop of blood, sweat, and tears. And the good news is that Jesus continues his ministry today in his church and in each of our lives—there is always a possibility of change when Jesus is around!

Here are a few thoughts that have reframed my thinking, reformed my heart, and reenergized my spirit in relationship to changing this dynamic.

A New Creation

> Therefore, if anyone is in Christ, the new creation has come: The old has gone, the new is here! (2 Corinthians 5:17)

There are times I feel like a new creation and seasons I don't. We may say or think, "But you don't know what I've done or thought. I don't feel like a new creation; I feel condemned or guilty much of the time; I'm broken. I've sinned, I've backed away from living for Jesus." Where do we turn during these seasons of life? To ourselves or Jesus?

The fact of the matter is this: Our identity lies in Jesus Christ—not in our production, our heritage, our good (or bad) deeds, but in Jesus. I've found over seventy-five terms in the Bible that identify me. When Jesus died on the cross and I accepted this in my baptism by faith, he gave me these identifiers. We have a choice to make—do we identify ourselves by our lives or as "in Christ"?

> This is what the LORD says:
> "Cursed is the one who trusts in man,
>   who draws strength from mere flesh

> *and whose heart turns away from the LORD.*
> *That person will be like a bush in the wastelands;*
>   *they will not see prosperity when it comes.*
> *They will dwell in the parched places of the desert,*
>   *in a salt land where no one lives.*
> *"But blessed is the one who trusts in the LORD,*
>   *whose confidence is in him.*
> *They will be like a tree planted by the water*
>   *that sends out its roots by the stream.*
> *It does not fear when heat comes;*
>   *its leaves are always green.*
> *It has no worries in a year of drought*
>   *and never fails to bear fruit."* (Jeremiah 17:5–8)

This is more than an intellectual exercise. Ask anyone going through recovery or in grief. When times are most difficult, mere words do not offer an identity. Jesus once said, "The work of God is this: to believe in the one he has sent" (John 6:29). The work of Christians is to truly *believe* and to act on their belief. I think the hard work of Christianity is to believe what Jesus has already told us. That is what this book is all about—connection to Jesus, through spiritual disciplines. It takes actual work. Here are two closing thoughts on the work of identity:

1. Vulnerability with others is essential. *Your mind is like a dangerous neighborhood—don't go there by yourself.* Be open with trusted friends. This takes a safe and confidential environment. There should be no gossip and no sharing others' difficulties without their permission. Ask for and expect confidentiality.

2. Replace lies with truth. Confront your false identities with the truth. *Memorize and meditate on Scripture.* This is a lost art but very biblical. *The Journey of the Soul* contains tremendous resources on how to meditate, spiritual formation, ruminating on Scripture, and much more!

    Embed your identity given to you from God by the cross.

With audacity, believe that you may not be who you think you are, because your identity lies in Christ. Our hope and prayer are that your time in this book will allow you space, knowledge, and encouragement to find approaches that help you to connect with God, follow Jesus, and listen to the Holy Spirit in refreshing and life-giving ways.

Kintsugi

Kintsugi is a form of Japanese art. The vessel above[5] has been broken and then repaired with gold inlays. When finished, it is more beautiful than before the brokenness, and it is stronger at the *very places it was broken.* Just like our lives: God rebuilds us stronger at our broken places.

The new creation for you may be this: We are all broken in different places. God redeems our brokenness by his grace and unending love for us and creates new life in our broken places.

Your life is an attraction to others *because of* (not in spite of) your broken pieces. You are a much stronger person because of the challenges and difficulties you've endured.

This is hard—why does life have to be so difficult? I don't know, but I do know that our challenges make us stronger people and are an attraction for others to follow. Our broken places are the very window people need to find God! Paul practiced this (twelve times in the books of 1 and 2 Corinthians Paul called himself "weak"). Where did Paul learn this lesson? From Jesus.

Jesus attracts us to him by his own weakness (2 Corinthians 13:4). Jesus once said: "And I, when I am lifted up from the earth, will draw all people to myself" (John 12:32). In Jesus' weakest

---

5. www.pexels.com, used with permission.

moment of life (being murdered on a cross) he draws us to him. Isn't that true for you? We are most drawn to Jesus because of the way he became weak for us. Could there be a greater demonstration of weakness than having people murder you for the murderers' sakes?

The difference between Paul and Jesus is this: Paul simply admitted what was true for him—he was weak. Jesus, on the other hand, *decided* to be weak for our sakes. He humbled himself (Philippians 2:8), had no place to sleep (Matthew 8:20), became poor for our sakes (2 Corinthians 8:9), and finally allowed himself to be unjustly killed. Weakness was Jesus' choice, and he made it with us in mind.

Practice Meditation: Three Sticks

This is a communion message I gave recently from a topic that has radically changed my life—the gentle and lowly heart of Jesus. As you begin to consider changes in your life and what God may have in mind for you as you practice spiritual disciplines, you may run into the "brick wall" of failure in your life. Try this meditation to leave your failures and sin in the place they belong—the heart of Jesus.

Imagine breaking these three Sticks:

- **A twig** – This stick represents the "easy" things God may have removed from your life as a Christian. For me, it was drinking and cursing. After many years of indulging in both to my (and others') harm, God simply removed them from my life. Poof... gone. What about you? What were some of the things God took care of for you? Most of us can list a few, and we are thankful for that!

- **A larger branch** – This larger piece of wood represents some of the more difficult things that we've been able to overcome over the years. Perhaps a bad habit, a character flaw, or other behavior or way of thinking that has changed in your life. Often this happens after study, prayer, mentoring, more prayer, maybe a recovery group, etc. Again, when we are able to overcome these kinds of issues, we are grateful to God for his work.

- **Now imagine a log, a big log** – Not the kind you can break over your knee or whittle down, but one that is big and thick. Kind of like those areas of your life that have not changed yet and, as you know yourself, may never change. Perhaps you've read books on this, you've listened to others who tried to help you, your spouse knows all about you in this area, or it has been there a long time—that log. Think about your life and some of the logs…with sin…shame…difficulties…memories…guilt… or character issues.

Now find one **big log** in your life… Do you have something in your mind? Please hold that image in your head and heart for a moment. Do you have one in mind? Good; if not, take a moment to think of one, **the toughest one.**

Now read Matthew 11:28–30.

"Come to me, all who labor and are heavy laden, and I will give you rest. Take my yoke upon you, and learn from me, for I am gentle and lowly in heart, and you will find rest for your souls. For my yoke is easy and my burden is light." (ESV)

This is the only place in the New Testament where you will find Jesus describing his own heart. He uses the words "gentle and lowly." Other translations use words like "humble," "meek," "mild," "free of pride" and "not arrogant."

Jesus, when he had the chance to describe his heart, could have used other words. He could have said, "I am challenging and convicting in heart," or "I am determined and passionate in heart," but instead, he calls himself gentle and lowly in heart. Ruminate on these words for a moment: "gentle and lowly." What images come to mind with gentle and lowly?

Now close your eyes. Take three deep breaths and exhale slowly. Relax your body and try to clear your mind and heart for a moment. Now…walk that LOG image you are holding in your mind…into the gentle and lowly heart of Jesus. Carefully and without judgment, hand that LOG over to Jesus.

When you do that, what do you find?

You find a gentle and humble heart—a heart that invites and attracts us.

A heart that takes on your burdens and sins.

When we are at our worst, Jesus is at his best—it is what he is made for.[6]

What do you hear?

Perhaps: "Lord, have mercy on me, a sinner". . .or maybe a simple plea like Peter's "Lord save me!" or. . .there is now no condemnation for those in Christ Jesus.

As we close this exercise, consider the joy you find in giving up that LOG. . . Leave your image behind, in the caring, gentle, and lowly heart of Jesus. Don't bring it back with you but leave it where it belongs, in his heart.

Now open your eyes.

This is what Jesus was created to be for us. We are to bring him our burdens, our worries, what we struggle with (1 Peter 5:7). When we bring our challenges to Jesus, we find a man who does not judge, but heals. And the areas he does not fully heal, he answers with gentleness, compassion, and care. A gently and lowly heart.

How to Use This Book

In this book you will find several passionate, caring, scholarly, professional, and devoted disciples of Jesus sharing God's heart for our souls. These chapters are an introduction to help you begin a journey of soul care. Here are a few thoughts as you begin:

- **Of course, these practices are not regulations commanded by God** to burden us, to prove our commitment, or requirements for salvation—they are gifts from God.

- **Be kind to yourself.** If Jesus has a compassionate,

---

6. Dane C. Ortlund, *Gentle and Lowly: The Heart of Christ for Sinners and Sufferers* (Wheaton, IL: Crossway, 2020).

gentle, and humble heart for us, shouldn't we do the same for ourselves? Practice kindness to yourself as you experience new adventures. Try not to judge yourself (or others)—just take this information as the grace of God, teaching you something new.

- **Think heart, emotions, connection.** While a cognitive approach to learning and drawing close to God is essential, let me encourage you to think heart, emotion, and relationship. God wants us to connect with him emotionally and relationally, with our heart. That is what we all want from our closest friends and spouses. To know and be known *relationally*.

- **Open your mind to something new.** Some of these ideas may challenge you. That is okay. We are called disciples because we are *learners*. We follow a man who deeply felt his walk with God. Jesus was not a robot who simply "did," but the Son of Man who experienced a deep, nuanced, joy-driven, exciting experiential relationship with his Father. We want the same for our lives.

- **Read what interests you.** You may want to hop around this book and not read it straight through. Leave it on a table to pick up later. Read and chew on one chapter, practice it, and then find another chapter to read. *This book can be viewed more like a handbook than one to read through and be done with.*

- **Practice. Experience this work.** Take time daily to do even a little bit of a lesson. This does not come quickly and easily. It takes work and practice. Allow yourself plenty of grace as you try out these disciplines. Try them on a walk. In the quietness of the early morning. During a hectic day at work. Do them alone or with a friend or in a small group setting. Before or after a meal. On the weekends or during the week. Plan a two-day retreat away from home to work on them. Just *experience* the gift of spiritual disciplines. You'll never be the same!

Using Resources

My people are destroyed from lack of knowledge. (Hosea 4:6)

I fly a lot to share mental health workshops with churches domestically and internationally. Due to chronic ear problems, I often experienced excruciating pain upon the airplane's descent. It got to a point where I had decided I might need to give up traveling and find something different to do.

So I began to seek help. Many internet searches and friends' advice took place. "Use gum! Try these earplugs, swallow often, snort this antihistamine, or take those little red pills." I tried them all, but nothing seemed to help. I began to despair. Then, while telling a nurse friend about my dilemma, she said, "Tim, do them all at once." That had never occurred to me. This happened a few years ago, and now I carry a little kit full of pills, earplugs, gum, and nasal spray, and using them all at once, it works! No more problem.

Resources are like that. Instead of looking for that one "magic pill" that solves everything, try as many resources as you can to help usher in your growth in these areas. Pay close attention to your body, mind, and spirit as you work on these practices. Listen to the way resources help you and try more of what works. At the end of most of the chapters, you will see a list of resources. If that chapter helped you, go further. Read another book or listen to a podcast to take your knowledge to the next level. Research indicates that resources are our #1 opportunity to facilitate change in our lives.[7] Take advantage of the expertise of others to move along your journey of connecting with God!

---

7. *The Heart & Soul of Change: Delivering What Works in Therapy* 2nd ed. Edited by Barry L Duncan PsyD, Dr Scott D Miller PH D, Bruce E Wampold, and Mark A Hubble.

CHAPTER ONE

Soul Care:
Finding Peace Through the
Use of Spiritual Disciplines

Byron Parson, PMP

Byron Parson is the author of *Walk This Way: The Spirit-Led Life*. He leads seekers in the pursuit of spiritual formation and has been a speaker, coach, and guide for those in pursuit of a closer, more intimate relationship with God for more than twenty years. He is married to his beautiful wife, Lauri. They have three amazing children, Blake, Nina, and daughter-in-law Elizabeth. Byron has been a disciple of Christ for forty years. He has provided pastoral leadership for groups of thousands, hundreds, fifties, and tens. Presently, Byron facilitates an online twelve-week interactive spiritual growth and renewal experience. He also provides train-the-trainer spiritual services for individual breakthrough and personal development. He employs: Immanuel Prayer, biblical meditation, lectio divina, emotional freedom techniques, and other modalities for spiritual development that allow the person to eliminate or decrease humanized thinking about an infinite God.

When we speak of "soul care," it is helpful to describe just what we mean by "soul." For the purposes of this chapter, "soul" is defined as the combination of everything that makes us who we are. Our soul is the totality of what makes us a living being. Author Nicholas Cash beautifully describes the makeup of our souls this way:[8]

> The body is the physical aspect of the soul. The mind is the cognitive aspect of the soul—that part of us that thinks, reasons, and plans. The spirit is the heart, the will, the longings and intentions of the soul.

---

8. https://prayer.asburyseminary.edu/what-is-soul-care/

This understanding of the soul is very important because it highlights the many and varied aspects of our being that constitute our souls, all of which require care and attention to function properly. The word "soul" is not just religious jargon. The term "soul" is meaningfully used in business every day. Did you know that when you get on a plane, the airline refers to you as a soul? Airline officials refer to their seated passengers as souls to distinguish them from bodies that are being transported in the cargo hold below to another city for burial. In the tragic event of a plane crash, the airline will need to report how many souls perished and how many souls survived.

So when we speak of soul care, we are talking about the proper care and maintenance of every aspect of who we are. Soul care involves the proper care and maintenance of our bodies. Soul care directs our minds to true and healthy thoughts and reflections. Similarly, proper soul care addresses the objects of our intentions and will.

It's no small thing to care for a soul. Am I right, all you moms out there?

It takes time, attention, energy, and resources to keep us all alive, healthy, and whole. Consider the offer and admonition God asserts through the prophet Isaiah:

> This is what the Sovereign LORD, the Holy One of Israel, says:
> "In repentance and rest is your salvation,
>   in quietness and trust is your strength,
>   but you would have none of it." (Isaiah 30:15)

The neglect of soul care, the unwillingness to quiet ourselves, keeps some aspects of salvation from being realized and made tangible in our lives. When we fail to quiet ourselves, there is a part of salvation available to us in the here and now that we cannot experience with our nonstop, frenetic lifestyles. Likewise, there is a rich experience of salvation that we forfeit and fail to experience when regular rhythms of rest elude us.

God promises through Isaiah a strength that accompanies our salvation, a fruit of quietness, rest, and trust. That strength may be manifest in a variety of ways, but one way is for sure: the strength to stand, to persevere. The strength to endure and not burn out. The strength to hold onto a quiet, meek, and gentle spirit. The capacity to not give way to bitterness and resentment as losses, disappointments, and unmet expectations accumulate in this broken world.

Jesus requires this strength when he calls us to go the extra mile, turn the other cheek, love our enemies, and do good to those who mistreat us. That's a supernatural strength. Many professing believers today don't have the strength to love their brothers who identify with a different political party. We desperately need this strength. We desperately need spiritual practices, rhythms of attention to God that position us to receive and continue in this strength. This takes time and attention.

The thought and effort dedicated to the care of a soul understandably cannot at the same time be devoted to productivity, advancement, development, etc. Soul care comes at a cost. Something's got to give. Fortunately, the cost of soul care is a bargain compared to the cost of neglecting our souls. Nonetheless, the time must be allocated. The attention must be given. The energy and effort must be expended. And the resources must be employed.

Given all the other things in life that compete for our time, attention, and energy, how do we insert or shove soul care into an already full and busy life? How will things get done? How do I keep up with life's demands? Where will I get the time?

For some people, soul care comes naturally; they don't even have to think about it. It's just how they go about life. That's not me. For most of us, soul care requires a considerable amount of focused intention. It doesn't come naturally to us. To us, soul care feels disruptive, unproductive, self-indulgent, and well, weird.

Soul Care Is a Skill

Like all skills, soul care skills are acquired through conscious effort or unconscious assimilation. Like most other skills in our lives, one's practice of soul care falls into one of four categories.

In 1969, management trainer Martin M. Broadwell recognized four stages of acquiring skills.[9] His teaching model is based on the

---

9. https://blog.dtssydney.com/in-a-nutshell-four-stages-of-competence

premise that our awareness of our own skills comes from both our conscious and our unconscious mind. Broadwell's stages are being:

1) unconsciously incompetent
2) consciously incompetent
3) consciously competent
4) unconsciously competent

These stages perfectly describe our experience and practice of soul care. Let's begin with Stage 1, being "unconsciously incompetent."

Some of us are not even aware that our souls need care. The subtle and sometimes not-so-subtle signals in our bodies and emotional states don't even register on our radars. We don't "feel" the need for soul care. Sometimes we feel things quite sharply but don't recognize them as the cries of our souls. Nor have we picked up from our families of origin, cultures, or schooling any practices that speak to the needs of our souls. Being unconsciously incompetent in the area of soul care, we don't know that we don't know what soul care is all about.

Let's move to Stage 2, being "consciously incompetent."

Some of us are aware of the need to practice soul care but have never acquired the skills. There is no rhythm of practices in our life that addresses the needs of our soul.

Regarding Stage 3, being "consciously competent":

For some of us, our practice of soul care is very much a conscious effort. We understand that our soul needs to be cared for, whether we feel the need tangibly or not. Like the minerals in our diet; for example, we don't have a taste for B12 consciously, but we know we need it and intentionally seek to include it in our diets or supplements.

And lastly, we come to Stage 4, being "unconsciously competent."

Here, we practice our soul care effortlessly, competently, and largely without even thinking about it. For the most part, we are just going about our business. We are largely unaware of the little ways we are monitoring our internal world and responding accordingly.

> **Question:** What stage best describes where you are when it comes to the regular practice of soul care in your life?

Now that we have established what we mean by the soul and understand that soul care is not intuitive to everyone, let's take a look at the relationship between soul care and the purposes of God.

Soul Care Is Inextricably Entwined with Our Salvation

From that time on Jesus began to explain to his disciples that he must go to Jerusalem and suffer many things at the hands of the elders, the chief priests and the teachers of the law, and that he must be killed and on the third day be raised to life.

Peter took him aside and began to rebuke him. "Never, Lord!" he said. "This shall never happen to you!"

Jesus turned and said to Peter, "Get behind me, Satan! You are a stumbling block to me; you do not have in mind the concerns of God, but merely human concerns." (Matthew 16:21–23)

Wow! Note to self: "Always make sure you have in mind the things of God."

Is soul care one of the "things of God?" Or is it merely a human invention? Is it an excuse to be lazy? Do we stop doing God's will on occasion to rest up and get refreshed so we can get back to God's will? These are important questions. Sincere believers and full-time ministers will not meaningfully practice soul care if they think it deters or in any way hinders God's calling on their lives.

I'm sure there are things labeled as soul care that are carnal and unspiritual. But biblically based soul care is our participation in the very salvation that God provides.

Practically speaking, soul care is a participation in Christ himself. It is the way we obey the scripture that says, "Work out your salvation with fear and trembling" (NIV). Soul care is a crucial part of God's redemptive plan. On a cosmic level, God's work includes the reversal of universal decay by the renewing of all creation.

On a personal level, God's activity in the world is to bring about humankind's salvation. That's a kind of renewing also, a reversal of sin and its corrosive effects. I know "salvation" is a religious word. For many people across the globe, salvation is synonymous with the forgiveness of sin. It is a pardon for the wrong that we have done and a reprieve from the punishment we deserve. That is marvelously true. It is a much bigger deal than we imagine. And on top of all that, forgiveness is but a fraction of what we have in salvation. The salvation that the death, burial, resurrection, ascension, and enthronement of Christ accomplished for you and me is far more than the forgiveness of sin alone. The salvation Christ extends to us is composed of everything needed to make us whole, enjoying life to the full (John 10:10).

The Apostle Peter describes this salvation in 1 Peter 1:8–9:

> *Though you have not seen him, you love him; and even though you do not see him now, you believe in him and are filled with an inexpressible and glorious joy, for you are receiving the end result of your faith, the salvation of your souls.*

What God intends to bring to us with his salvation is "an inexpressible and glorious joy." The Apostle Paul declares that this salvation brings about a peace that passes all understanding (Philippians 4:7).

By salvation, we mean the sum of God's actions on our behalf to rescue us from the things that erode or crush our spirits, minds, bodies, and relationships. The things that suppress and sideline inexpressible joy, and peace that passes understanding. As you can see, salvation is much more than the final destination of our disembodied souls. Being saved is not a transaction by which our souls are moved from a "lost hook" in heaven and placed on the "saved hook" in heaven. Salvation is a rescue mission.

The result of God's actions to bring us out of the kingdom of darkness and into the kingdom of the Son that he loves is often summed up in the English word "saved." But remember, being saved is a great deal more than being forgiven. The Greek word often used by the New Testament writers that is regularly translated as "saved" is *sozo*. An example of this is found in Acts 4:12: "Salvation is found in no one else, for there is no other name under heaven given to mankind by which we must be saved."

The interesting thing is that this same word *sozo* is translated as:

Healed
Delivered
Blessed
Prospered
Protected
Set apart
Made whole

Apparently, our salvation is something that happens not just in the hereafter but also in the here and now! God's salvation is felt; it is discernible, even palpable.

Question: Does the inclusion of healed, delivered, blessed, prospered, protected, set apart, and made whole change your view of what it means to be saved?

When I need to change a long-held impression I have had about a matter, I make a habit of going back to the source and its original use in context. Here is an excerpt from Strong's Concordance[10] that you might find helpful.

It describes sozo as follows:

sōzō: to save
Original Word: σῴζω
Part of Speech: Verb
Transliteration: *sōzō*
Phonetic Spelling: (sode'-zo)
Definition: to save
Usage: I save, heal, preserve, rescue.
sōzō (from sōs, "safe, rescued") – properly, deliver out of danger

and into safety; used principally of God rescuing believers from the penalty and power of sin—and into his provisions (safety).

(*sózō*) is the root of: /*sōtér* ("Savior"), /*sōtéría* ("salvation") and the adjectival form, /*sōtérion* (what is "saved/rescued from destruction and brought into divine safety").

This rich, multifaceted gift of salvation is not just dropped upon us from above. Neither is this salvation something for which we labor, or strive to earn. But rather, this salvation is something that God has ordained for us to receive and experience through our participation in Christ. Soul care is inextricably entwined with our participation in Christ.

In many ways, soul care is how we unwrap and experience the riches of God's salvation. For although we have already been given everything we need for life and godliness, inexpressible joy, and peace, we rarely if ever feel it. It's as though this precious gift has landed in a field strewn with the weeds of erroneous beliefs and the rocks of maladaptive behaviors.

At the core of all soul care practices are the reflection on and participation in the nature of God. After all, regardless of the practice in which we choose to engage, the goal is to be refreshed, renewed, restored, and transformed by attending to and attuning with God.

That's so intimate. So close. So raw. There is no way we will give ourselves so completely and unreservedly to God unless we find him to be safe, attractive, and desirable. Our hearts must be persuaded of God's good and desirable intentions toward us before we will truly come to him and rest in his presence. Again, the Apostle Paul helps us here with a truth he proclaimed to the church in Rome. He says in Romans 14:17:

> *For the kingdom of God is not a matter of eating and drinking, but of righteousness, peace and joy in the Holy Spirit.*

---

10. *Strong's Exhaustive Concordance of the Bible,* generally known as *Strong's Concordance,* is a Bible concordance, an index of every word in the King James Version (KJV), constructed under the direction of James Strong. Strong first published his concordance in 1890 while professor of exegetical theology at Drew Theological Seminary.

Have you ever really thought about what Paul, the great sufferer for Christ Jesus, is saying here? Powerful emotions are central to and at the foundation of our salvation. Joy is an emotion. Peace is an emotion. Even the righteousness referred to in Romans 14:17 is a sense or feeling of orderliness, the settled feeling that things are as they should be. God rescues us from a kingdom of darkness where we are fractured, disordered, and oppressed. We feel the difference. Our salvation is palpable. Our salvation is not merely a matter of cognitive understanding but more a visceral experience. Salvation makes a difference you can feel. And not just any old feeling. Pressure is a feeling. Pain is a feeling. Nervousness is a feeling. Paul says that salvation feels like joy. It feels like peace. Salvation feels right, like things are as they should be.

In this passage, Paul is calling the brothers and sisters in Rome to use the Holy Spirit emotions of joy, peace, and righteousness as barometers for the condition of their souls. Paul's ministry metric, his definition of success in ministry, is the presence of Spirit-kindled joy, peace, and orderliness (righteousness) experienced in the lives of the believers. I have personally experienced the reality of the Spirit's holy emotions in some profound ways. Here is a recent example:

I was driving down the westbound 210 freeway through the San Gabriel mountains in Los Angeles, commuting to work on a Thursday morning. As I drove, I noticed a thought that had been circling in my mind all morning. It was sparked by a book I was studying on the perils of accepting the praise of human beings.

And the thought that wouldn't let me go was, "Just how many things in my life have been motivated by the praise of people; some 'attaboy,' some recognition, some advancement, title, raise, or promotion, a request to speak, teach, or facilitate; some acknowledgement of value and accomplishment? The recognition that something was exceptional in my life."

I was honestly stumped by the idea of how to go forward without pursuing any of these things, because my whole life seemed to have been driven by the pursuit of someone's else's praise or acknowledgement. From my elementary school days of going after gold stars, to my years in the Boy Scouts earning merit badges, to my high school and college years aiming for top grades, and then to my work life striving for advancement and promotions.

As I drove, suddenly an image popped in my mind. It was like a bleak and desolate Old West scene with drab mountains in the distance and tumbleweed rolling across a lonely dirt road. That image symbolized my outlook of a life without all the praise, acknowledgements, and accolades bestowed by others.

So I prayed while I drove, "Lord, give me a vision of what my life would be seeking only your praise. What would my life look like without personally planning and arranging for those moments of praise from people? Without those celebrated moments, the future seems empty and bleak."

And in that very moment, God reminded me, "You know, Byron, the very best things in your life, over the course of your whole life, were not things that you prayed for, longed for, or sought after. The very best things in your life you didn't even know existed until I brought them to you."

In an instant, my mind was flooded with images of treasured moments and people in my life: meeting my wife, the birth of my children, enchanted moments in nature, festive holidays, amazing people, and on and on.

I was overwhelmed by how true it was. Not only had the best things in my life so far been orchestrated, planned, and brought about by God, but that would be my future as well. I had nothing to worry about. My future is not bleak and empty, but rich and bright. The goodness of God toward me would not only continue, but increase.

As I cruised down the highway, I felt the lump in my throat and the familiar sting in my eyes as tears of joy welled up and spilled over onto my cheeks. God is so good. I could hardly contain it. I laughed out loud. I grinned from ear to ear. I placed one hand over my mouth while the other gripped the steering wheel. I thought quickly, *I can't have this kind of prayer time and drive at the same time. This is dangerous.*

From that moment, my heart was settled. Goodness and love to follow me all the days of my life. I was now able to rest in the goodness of God, excited about my future; not needing the praise or fearing the rejection of human beings. God's goodness had produced in me an inexpressible and glorious joy.

Transformation Is the Fruit of What We Behold

You will receive many helpful tools and practices throughout this book regarding soul care for you and those you love. You will find yourself beholding God as he truly brings forth life-giving emotions that withstand the momentary difficulties we face. Allow me to share just one soul-care truth with you here: conversational prayer.

Conversational Prayer

This spiritual practice moves from monologue offered to God to a mutually responsive dialogue with God. Like most spiritual disciplines, conversational prayer is best experienced in a space of solitude and silence. We want to add to that a period of praise and thanksgiving. Having consciously entered God's presence (I say consciously because we know that God is always there) we bring before God a scripture that we would like him to illuminate for us or a life issue for which we seek his perspective and direction.

The following account happened on a sunny Sunday morning. I was alone in the apartment. My wife and kids would not be back for several hours. We were expecting a large communion dinner crowd later that afternoon. Many preparations had already been made, but there remained more for me to do than usual. I was seated in the living room in a brown leather recliner. I meditated with soft instrumental music playing in the background for about an hour. With my journal in hand to capture any impressions, I raised the following question to God and sat poised to notice what he had for me in reply.

Here is my journal entry from June 18, 2018:

>...God, how can I not be anxious and stay relational all day? Not problem-solve in having everything ready at 3 pm. Not be in performance mode where I'm driven by people's responses

to the house, food, and communion thoughts.

How can I just be myself? Can God use the most genuine things about me to influence the people in the group for the Lord?

His response was, "I have formed every aspect of your being for the display of my splendor: every hair that remains, every mole and freckle. I have carved every line in your face. I made your eyes and delight in the years they reveal. Every bit of stubble and the coloration is by my design. Even your hair line and the fullness of your face I will use for the display of my splendor. So let your light shine. Be fully present and out front. Give each person your unrivaled attention and the warmth of your smile in full affection.

"Embrace with tenderness. Touch with care. Share with unbridled enthusiasm whatever geeky, nerdy, intellectual interests, passions, convictions you may have, including conspiracy theories. If there is something you want them to know, tell them. If something you want to teach, teach it. If a point to make, make it. Be fully on display—you are my craftsmanship; you reflect my glory. Delight in it and take pleasure in the work of my hands.

"Tell the people what happened here one Sunday morning in June. I am the Lord."

I recall over a period of hours feeling God's love wash all over me. I felt waves of joy roll all through my body. I laughed. I cried. It was as if God was a mere few inches from me declaring his love and affection. I felt tingly all over. I felt lighter, as if a great burden had been lifted off me. I sat for some time while the sensations of the moment slowly dissipated.

Eventually I got up. There were still things to get done. I wasn't sure exactly what I was going to say at the communion dinner. But one thing I knew for sure and have not doubted since: *God loves me and is delighted with me, the work of his hands.*

Resources

E. James Wilder, James G. Friesen, Anne Bierling, Rick Koepcke, and Maribeth Poole, *Living from the Heart Jesus Gave You* (East Peoria, IL: Shepherd's House, 2016).

Peter Scazzero, *The Emotionally Healthy Leader* (Grand Rapids, MI: Zondervan, 2015).

Henry T. Blackaby, *Experiencing God: Knowing and Doing the Will of God* (Nashville, TN: B&H).

Jan Johnson, *When the Soul Listens: Finding Rest and Direction in Contemplative Prayer* (Colorado Springs, CO: NavPress, 2017).

Peter Lord, *Hearing God: An Easy-to-Follow, Step-by-Step Guide to Two-Way Communication with God* (Bloomington, MN: Chosen, 2011).

Dallas Willard, *The Divine Conspiracy: Rediscovering Our Hidden Life in God* (New York, NY: HarperCollins, 2009).

Dr. Marcus Warner and Jim Wilder, *The Solution of Choice: Four Good Ideas That Neutralized Western Christianity* (New York, NY: Primedia, 2018).

Byron Parson, *Walk This Way: The Spirit-Led Life* (self-published, 2016).

CHAPTER TWO

Spiritual Bible Reading—
What Is It?

Dr. G. Steve Kinnard, DMin

G. Steve Kinnard, DMin from Drew University, is dean of the Bible department at the Rocky Mountain School of Ministry and Theology and an adjunct professor of Bible at Lincoln Christian University. He serves as a teacher and evangelist with the New York City Church of Christ and has trained congregational teachers across the continent of Africa. Steve has published more than twenty books, including *King Jesus, Getting the Most from the Bible,* and a novel entitled *Our Struggle.* He recently finished translating the Greek New Testament into English, in a work entitled *The King Jesus Translation.*

With great curiosity we search out the thoughts of men, and yet we neglect the thoughts of God. One word of the good news of the gospel is more precious than all the other books in the world put together—it is the source of all truth.

We ought to listen with such love, such faith, such adoration, to the words of Jesus Christ in the gospel! From this moment forward let us say to him, along with Saint Peter, "Lord, to whom shall we go? You have the words of eternal life."[11]   —Francis Fenelon, mystic

How can we saturate our minds with Christ? There is but one way to get a true picture of him. This is to read his life in the four Gospels so often that we know it by heart.[12]   —Frank Laubach, prayer warrior

---

11. Francis Fenelon, *The Complete Fenelon* (Brewster, MA: Paraclete Press, 2012), 89–90.

12. Frank C. Laubach, *Prayer: The Mightiest Force in the World* (New York, NY: Fleming H. Revell Company, [n.d.].), 74.

> The Bible is primarily a book not of information but of formation, not merely a book to be analyzed, scrutinized, and discussed but a sacred book to nurture us, to unify our hearts and minds, and to serve as a constant source of contemplation.[13]   —Henri Nouwen, devotional writer

I opened this chapter with the words of Francis Fenelon. His statement is my favorite quote concerning Bible study. I especially love this line: "One word of the good news of the gospel is more precious than all the other books in the world put together—it is the source of all truth." Do you believe Fenelon's statement? Do you believe that "one word of the good news of the gospel is more precious than all the other books in the world put together?" If so, is your belief reflected in practice? Do you spend time meditating upon God's word?

I love to read. Reading is good for you. It feeds your mind. Reading isn't as popular as it once was; we live in a video age. But videos don't feed your mind like reading.

I read all kinds of books. Business books, novels, theological books, martial arts books, magazines, the *New York Times*. But of all the books I read, nothing feeds my spirit like the Bible.

Take a moment and answer these questions:

1. Who is your favorite singer?
2. How many of their songs can you name?
3. What is your favorite sports team?
4. How many players can you name from that team (both past and present players)?
5. How many parables of Jesus can you name?
6. What are the names of the twelve Apostles?

The point of the exercise is to demonstrate that when we really like something, it becomes a part of us. I have memorized Johnny Cash songs without even trying. How? Repetition. I listened to the

---

13. Henri Nouwen, *Spiritual Formation: Following the Movements of the Spirit* (New York, NY: HarperCollins, 2010).

songs so much that they became a part of me. The same with the Beatles. I can hear the first few notes of a Beatles song and name the song. I know most of their songs by heart. I never sat down and tried to memorize one of their songs. It happened over time because I listened to their music so often.

Is the same true of God's word? Have I read it so much, repeated its lines and phrases so often, that it has become a part of my heart? Have I studied the Word so often that I know the lines upon the page?

Over time, if we read the Bible and meditate upon its words, phrases, sentences, paragraphs, stories, poems, parables, proverbs, and psalms, then it will become a part of who we are. We will find that the Bible will sink deep into our psyche. We will discover that the Bible is no longer just a book we read, but it is the living word of God that dwells in our hearts.

This is the point of Bible study. In Bible study we don't seek to master the Bible; we seek to allow the Bible to master us.

Jesus and Bible Study

How deeply did Jesus know Scripture? Really well. Let's face it, he was the incarnate Word of God (John 1:1, 14). Jesus quoted Scripture throughout his ministry. He quoted 78 times from the Hebrew Scriptures. He quoted from the Pentateuch 28 times. He quoted from 34 of the 39 Old Testament books. Do you know which books he didn't quote from?[14]

As a young boy of twelve, he baffled the Jewish teachers at the temple with his understanding of Scripture (Luke 2). He won a victory over Satan in the desert by quoting Scripture (Matthew 4). He rebuked the Sadducees because they failed to know the Scriptures or the power of God (Matthew 22:29). When the Pharisees approached him to ask about divorce and remarriage, Jesus asked them, "Haven't you read?" (Matthew 19:3–6). When he cleansed the temple, he used Scripture to explain his actions (Matthew 21:12–13).

Jesus had a profound respect for Scripture. In John 10:35 he said, "The Scripture cannot be broken." In Matthew 5:17 Jesus said,

---

14. Jesus did not quote from *Ezra, Nehemiah, Song of Songs, Ecclesiastes,* and *Esther*

"Do not think that I have come to abolish the Law or the Prophets; I have not come to abolish them but to fulfill them." In the very next verse he stated, "I tell you the truth, until heaven and earth disappear, not the smallest letter, not the least stroke of a pen, will by any means disappear from the Law until everything is accomplished."

In Luke 4:14–31, Jesus begins his ministry. He does so by reading Scripture. Luke 4:16 reads, "He went to Nazareth, where he had been brought up, and on the Sabbath day he went into the synagogue, as was his custom. And he stood up to read." Nazareth was a backwater village of around 100 people. Some scholars say that Nazareth was made up of a sectarian cult who believed they were the *netzer*, the bud of the plant of King David. In other words, these Netzerene believed that the Messiah would come from their number.

It was Jesus' custom to go to the synagogue on the sabbath. When it came time for the reading of Scripture, the ruler of the local synagogue normally asked a worthy person to read from the Scriptures and to make a comment on the reading. Since Jesus had been teaching in towns around Nazareth, it makes sense that the synagogue official asked him to read from the Scriptures. Luke 4:17–19 reads:

> The scroll of the prophet Isaiah was handed to him. Unrolling it, he found the place where it is written:
> "The Spirit of the Lord is on me,
> > because he has anointed me
> > to preach good news to the poor.
> He has sent me to proclaim freedom for the prisoners
> > and recovery of sight for the blind,
> to set the oppressed free,
> > to proclaim the year of the Lord's favor."

Jesus knew exactly what he wanted he read. He unrolled the scroll and started reading. He chose a messianic text, Isaiah 61. Jesus knew Scripture. He picked a text that talked about the year of the Lord's favor. Then he said the text was fulfilled in their hearing. In Luke 4:18–19, Jesus declares:

> *"The Spirit of the Lord is on me,*
> *because he has anointed me*
> *to preach good news to the poor.*
> *He has sent me to proclaim freedom for the prisoners*
> *and recovery of sight for the blind,*
> *to set the oppressed free,*
> *to proclaim the year of the Lord's favor."*

Jesus picked just the right passage to deliver the message he wanted to get across. He knew Scripture.

Spiritual Bible Reading—Listening for God's Voice in the Scriptures

Bible study is an art, not a science. It is a personal art. What I mean is that each person is fed by the Bible in different ways. To get the most out of reading your Bible, you have to approach Bible reading from a spiritual perspective. I call this spiritual Bible reading.

Most schools teach us how to read to gain information. This is known as informational reading. Spiritual Bible reading is counterintuitive. It is not what we are taught in school. It doesn't come naturally. We read looking for details, but not for the Spirit. Most people have to learn how to read the Bible spiritually.

Before we move on to discuss the "how" of spiritual Bible reading, let's take a moment to look at the "why" of reading the Bible. Why is it important to read God's word? There are many answers to this question. Let's look at a few of them.

Whether you are a young Christian, an old Christian, or a non-Christian who wants to have a relationship with God, great Bible study is the key to getting close and staying close to him. If you don't have a relationship with God and are just beginning to get serious about learning more about him, then dig into the Bible and let it teach you about God. If you are a part of the church and want to grow as a disciple, then part of the process of spiritual maturity is learning from the Scriptures. If you have been a disciple for years and years and desire to keep the edge you had when you first became a disciple, then God's word will help you stay sharp. To say it plainly, a steady diet of God's word is essential for spiritual growth. If we do not have deep, meaningful Bible study, we will not do well spiritually.

The first key to having great, life-changing Bible study is to appreciate the great gift that God has given you by giving you his word. You need to be grateful that you have the living word of God at your fingertips. You must hold the Bible in awe. I went around my house and counted, and we have sixty-three copies of the Bible in our house. We have it in Hebrew, Greek, Russian, Hindi, Spanish, Latin, and Samaritan.[15] We have children's Bibles, poet's Bibles, New Testaments, Old Testaments, small print, large print, computer versions, cloth bound, leather bound, the Bible on video, the Bible on compact disc, and everything in between. We have it in numerous English translations: the Revised Standard Version, the New Revised Standard Version, the New International Version, the King James Version, the New King James Version, the Cotton Patch Version, The Jerusalem Bible, the American Standard Version, the New American Standard Bible, the Singing Version, The Message, the Tanakh, the Living Oracles edition, the English Standard Version, the Messianic Jewish edition, and many more. The more used, marked, and worn it becomes, the more valuable it is.

How much do you appreciate the Bible? If you are uncertain, ask yourself a few simple questions: How much do you read the Bible? Do you know how to find your way around the Bible? Is your Bible underlined and marked up from use? Have you had studies in your Bible that have changed your life?

We need to appreciate the Word. We don't hold many things sacred in the International Churches of Christ. I think that is good. Although many religious groups consider baptism a sacrament and have all types of traditions that surround it, we baptize people any place, any time. We baptize in baptisteries, water fountains, horse troughs, swimming pools, rivers, lakes, oceans, bathtubs, or Jacuzzis. That's good. The place and time are not important. The person

---

15. I purchased the Samaritan Penteteuch on Mt. Gerizim in Nablus, Palestine from a Samaritan grocer while I was living in Jerusalem in 1998. I am one of a handful of people with a personal copy of this book. I can't read a word of it, but I love it just the same.

simply must understand what is happening when they are baptized. We do not have any "Holy Grails" in the church. That's fine. If we were to adopt one "holy," one "sacred," item in our church, I suggest that it should be our Bibles (notice I said "if"). We need to treat the Bible with reverence, respect, and awe.

I'll never forget a trip that my wife and I took to Bombay, India (now Mumbai) in the late 1980s. We went there for a campaign that the Bombay church was hosting. We went across the enormous city of Bombay asking people to study the Bible. As I was knocking doors, I met a young man from the Sikh religion, and we became good friends. We talked daily for the two weeks that I was there. When I was about to leave, he presented me with two gifts. One was a dagger from the Sikh holy temple in Amistar that was very special to him. Another was a copy of some of the sacred writings of the Sikh religion. His father was present when he gave me these gifts. His father was a little upset that his son gave me these items. He considered them sacred. His father asked me to do one thing for him. Since the writings were sacred to him, he asked me not to pack them in a suitcase that contained shoes. To him, it was disrespectful to place the sacred writings next to items that were worn on the feet. This was his way of paying respect to his sacred writings.

Modern Judaism also considers its Torah scrolls sacred. These scrolls are placed in a special box in the front of synagogues. The rabbi is not to touch these scrolls with his hands. The scrolls are wrapped around a pole with handles so they can be unrolled. The rabbi reads the scroll by pointing at the words with a special rod so that his fingers will not touch the parchment. When the scrolls become old and tarnished, they are buried in the ground as a sign of respect.

I'm not suggesting that we adopt this type of behavior with our Bibles. But I must admit I was once offended by a brother whom I saw using the Bible as a footstool. I asked him to not use his Bible to prop up his feet. That just didn't seem proper to me.

We can take the Bible for granted. We should realize that it is a recent phenomenon for average people to have a copy of the Scriptures. With Gutenberg's invention of the printing press in 1455, the

Bible was mass-produced for the first time. Before that time, most manuscripts were copied by hand. But even with the invention of the printing press, only the wealthy could afford a copy of the Bible. For centuries, the Catholic Church did not want its members to read the Bible. They believed that reading and interpreting the Scriptures should be left to the priests. John Wycliffe translated the Bible into English. William Tyndale later improved upon Wycliffe by translating the Bible into an English that was more easily understood. Martin Luther translated the Bible into German for everyone to read.

How did the Catholic Church react to these translations? It found Tyndale guilty of heresy and demanded that all his editions of the Bible be destroyed. They did such a thorough job of destroying Tyndale's Bibles that only two original editions are in existence today. William Tyndale was burned at the stake for heresy. The Catholic Church also found John Wycliffe guilty of heresy. Wycliffe was already dead when the priests pronounced him guilty of heresy. This did not deter his prosecutors; they simply dug up his dead body and burned it at the stake. Many people have given their lives so that we could have the Bible in our homes. We should never take the Bible for granted.

Spiritual Bible Reading—How?

It is important to read the Bible. It is equally important to learn to read the Bible correctly. When we read the Bible, we need to listen for God's voice. We need to learn how to read the Bible in a spiritual way.

Throughout school we are taught how to read informationally. We read to gain information. We read to gain knowledge. We are taught to ask questions like:

- Who are the main characters?
- What is the plot?
- What are the major themes? What are the minor themes?
- How does the author use symbolism?
- Most importantly, what do I need to know to pass the test?

When we read for information, we read trying to master the text. We conjugate the verbs and diagram the sentences. We look for subject, verbs, and modifiers.

We can do the same with the Bible. We can approach it like it's a textbook and try to master it. But that's not the best way to read the Bible. Someone once said, "We don't read to master the Word—we read to let the Word master us." Amen. That's a different approach to the Bible. Are you reading the Bible to master the Word or are you allowing the Word to master you?

We have to learn to read the Bible differently from how we have been taught to read literature. We are schooled to read literature to gather information. Make no mistake, it is helpful to read the Bible informationally. It is much better than not reading it at all. But there is a better approach to Bible study: spiritual Bible reading. When we read the Bible spiritually, we read it listening for the voice of God.

When we read the Bible for spiritual formation, we need to ask a different set of questions. We ask:

- Not just, who is the main character, but what character change can I make after reading this passage?

- Not only, what is the plot, but ask, God, how are you plotting out my life? What is your course for my life today, this week, this month, this year?

- Not just, what is the major theme, but what theme can I use from this Bible reading to motivate me to live for Jesus today?

The Bible is unlike every other book. It is the Holy Spirit's book. We know that the Holy Spirit produced the Bible; 2 Peter 1:20–21 reads, "Above all, you must understand that no prophecy of Scripture came about by the prophet's own interpretation. For prophecy never had its origin in the will of man, but men spoke from God as they were carried along by the Holy Spirit." Since the Holy Spirit gave us the Word, doesn't it make sense that the Holy Spirit is on every page of the word of God? Therefore, when we read the Bible, we need to find God's Spirit on every page.

I'm not saying that when we read the Bible, we need to jettison our intellect. The Bible is an intellectually stimulating book. What I am saying is that our primary object in reading the Bible should be that we feed our spirit, our soul.

1 Samuel 3:1–10 gives us an interesting phrase that I like to remember when I study the Bible. This is the story of Eli and Samuel. Samuel's mother, Hannah, dropped off Samuel at the temple to be trained by Eli. During the night, Samuel hears a voice whispering to him. Here is the story:

> The boy Samuel ministered before the LORD under Eli. In those days, the word of the LORD was rare; there were not many visions.
>
> One night Eli, whose eyes were becoming so weak that he could barely see, was lying down in his usual place. The lamp of God had not yet gone out, and Samuel was lying down in the temple of the LORD, where the ark of God was. Then the LORD called Samuel.
>
> Samuel answered, "Here I am." And he ran to Eli and said, "Here I am; you called me."
>
> But Eli said, "I did not call; go back and lie down." So he went and lay down.
>
> Again the LORD called, "Samuel!" And Samuel got up and went to Eli and said, "Here I am; you called me."
>
> "My son," Eli said, "I did not call; go back and lie down."
>
> Now Samuel did not yet know the LORD: The word of the LORD had not yet been revealed to him.
>
> A third time the LORD called, "Samuel!" And Samuel got up and went to Eli and said, "Here I am; you called me."
>
> Then Eli realized that the LORD was calling the boy. So Eli told Samuel, "Go and lie down, and if he calls you, say, 'Speak, LORD, for your servant is listening.'" So Samuel went and lay down in his place.
>
> The LORD came and stood there, calling as at the other times, "Samuel! Samuel!"
>
> Then Samuel said, "Speak, for your servant is listening."

Eli told Samuel to say to the voice, "Speak, for your servant is listening." When we read the Bible, we are listening to the voice of

God. We should respond by saying, "Speak, for your servant is listening." I wrote this phrase in the front of my Bible. When I open my Bible, I want to be reminded to say, "Speak, for your servant is listening."

When we read the Bible, we need to be "all ears." We need to listen intently to the Word. We need to listen for that one word or that one phrase that will carry us throughout the day.

Bible study should always be accompanied by prayer. Prayer opens our hearts to see what God wants us to see from his word. Karl Barth said, "Prayer without study would be empty. Study without prayer would be blind."

Spiritual Bible Reading—How to Read Spiritually

Now that we have discussed the nature of spiritual Bible reading, let's look at how to practice this art. We will begin with four foundational steps to read the Bible spiritually, then we will move on to talk about some practical matters in this important spiritual discipline.

Four Steps to Spiritual Bible Reading

Richard Foster gives four steps to spiritual Bible reading. These steps are: Repetition, Concentration, Comprehension, and Reflection. I have a few things to say about each of these steps.

1. Repetition

Repetition is the mother of all skill. The more we do something, the better we become at that skill. When you do something often enough, it becomes a part of you. It becomes who you are.

When I studied Kung Fu, we learned various defenses to attacks. We repeated these defensive actions over and over until they became natural to us. Over time, anything that you constantly repeat becomes a part of who you are. Have you ever read a book over and over to a child? Eventually, that child knows the book by heart. It seems as though they are reading the book along with you (although the child doesn't know how to read). The child has learned the book through repetition.

Richard Foster describes repetition, writing:

> Repetition is a way of regularly channeling the mind in a specific direction, thus ingraining habits of thought. Repetition has received something of a bad name today. It is important, however, to realize that sheer repetition without even understanding what is being repeated does affect the inner mind.[16]

Repetition isn't bad. It is neutral. It can be used to memorize Scripture or to help focus on concepts that we want to become a part of our lives. If used in the right way, repetition is a learning mechanism that can help us internalize the word of God until it becomes a natural part of our lives.

We are the habits that we perform every day. It is important that we have spiritual habits that help shape who we are and who we become. Paul Tournier writes:

> Everything is habit in biology, and habits are created only by means of repetition. Experiments have shown how much of our behavior is determined by the mental images to which our minds are constantly returning. If we bring our minds back again and again to God, we shall by the same inevitable law be gradually giving the central place to God, not only in our inner selves, but also in our practical everyday lives.[17]

Good habits are good for you. Good spiritual habits are good for the spirit. Thoughtful repetition in Bible study can help us focus on deep truths until those truths become a part of our lives.

2. Concentration

Reading just to read isn't really helpful. We must get something out of our reading. That something might be inspiration, encouragement, or yes, even pleasure. I love to read for pleasure. I've read Tolkien's *Lord of the Rings* trilogy over and over, and each time is just as enjoyable as the last. But just to sit and read words

---

16. R.J. Foster, *Celebration of Discipline: The Path to Spiritual Growth* (United Kingdom: HarperCollins, 1988), 65.

17. Foster, *Celebration of Discipline*, 66.

and sentences without getting anything out of it is a waste of time. When we read, we need to concentrate.

Richard Foster describes the benefits of concentration. He writes:

> Concentration centers the mind. It focuses the attention on the thing being studied. The human mind has incredible ability to concentrate. It is constantly receiving thousands of stimuli, every one of which it is able to store in its memory banks while focusing on only a few. This natural ability of the brain is enhanced when with singleness of purpose we center our attention upon a desired object of study.[18]

In order to focus, we must rid ourselves of distractions. For example, I love reading and I love watching football, but I can't do both at the same time.

Sometimes you can block out distractions. I've learned how to sit in the middle of a crowded room and block out everything around me so I can focus on what I'm reading. I can do this in an airport or at Starbucks. But if there is a single conversation going on next to me, then it is difficult to concentrate. Best to get up and move instead of reading without concentration.

What's the point here? If you are going to get the most out of your Bible study, you need to get rid of distractions that steal your focus. Everyone is different. For me, I can read with jazz music or classical music in the background. For others, that would be impossible. I can read when there is a golf tournament on television, but I can't read when there is a football game on TV. I need to choose to turn off the TV or close the book. You have to make these choices all the time. Get rid of the distractions that keep you from concentrating on the text. Read with a purpose.

3. Comprehension

We need to understand what we are reading. We need to concentrate, but we also need to determine the meaning of the text.

---

18. Foster, *Celebration of Discipline*, 66.

We need to ascertain what the author wants to communicate to us. In our postmodern world, some scholars say it is impossible to determine what the author meant in a text. Is it? I've written these words, and you are reading. I have no doubt that you understand what I have written. When you drive, you understand that a stop sign means "stop." If you run the sign and are pulled over by a police officer, would you say, "I wasn't sure of the meaning of 'stop.'" The officer might give you a breathalyzer test at that point. We communicate through words all day long. Truth can be communicated through words. When we read the Bible, we need to look for the meaning of the text.

Richard Foster states:

> Comprehension leads to insight and discernment. It provides the basis for a true perception of reality. When we not only repeatedly focus the mind in a particular direction, centering our attention on the subject, but understand the 'what' we are studying, we reach a new level.[19]

When you approach the text, ask certain questions about it. Who wrote this? To whom was it written? Where was the audience who received the text? What circumstances prompted its writing? What is the meaning of the text? How can I apply what I've learned to my life?

Read to understand the text. Comprehend the passage. Discern what the author meant to say. Place yourself in the context of the first hearers of the text. What would the text have meant to them as they listened to it for the first time? When we read with comprehension, when we dig deep into the passage and discover meaning, we find truth that feeds our souls.

4. Reflection

As we read, we concentrate to comprehend the author's meaning in the text. After we read, we reflect. Reflection is something that makes us different from animals. We don't just respond to

---

19. Foster, *Celebration of Discipline*, 66.

stimuli like an animal. As humans, we have the ability to reflect and make choices. Many texts call for a decision. Other texts inspire us to think about how we should live our lives. I just finished reading Victor Hugo's *Les Misérables*. This incredible novel tells the story of a priest who befriends an ex-convict. The priest's kindness transforms the life of the convict. Throughout this epic story, Hugo writes about the social injustices of early nineteenth-century Europe. As I read the novel, I was forced to think about the social inequity that still exists in the world today. Hugo made me look at the faces of the "miserable ones" in his society and transfer those faces to the twenty-first century. His writing called for reflection. I love when a book makes me meditate upon grand themes like grace, justice, and equality.

The Bible is a book written to cause us to reflect, ruminate, and meditate. God wants us to internalize the Bible so that our lives are transformed through his word. This is the point of reflection. Richard Foster writes, "To reflect, to ruminate, on the events of our time will lead us to the inner reality of those events. Reflection brings us to see things from God's perspective. In reflection we come to understand not only our subject matter, but ourselves."[20]

Reflection is the toughest and most costly aspect of reading the text. It doesn't always happen quickly or easily. It often takes time for us to understand what the text is calling us to do. Elizabeth O'Conner writes:

> To take a book of the Bible, to immerse oneself in it and to be grasped by it, is to have one's life literally revolutionized. This requires study and the training of attention. The student stays with it through barren day after barren day, until at last the meaning is clear, and transformation happens in his life.[21]

In reflection, we aren't trying to grasp the text; we are allowing the text to grasp us. We aren't attempting to master the text; we allow the text to master us. This is the toughest step of reading, but it is also the most rewarding.

20. Foster, *Celebration of Discipline*, 66.
21. lizabeth O'Connor, *Search for Silence* (Waco, Tx: Word Books, 1971).

Practical Matters

Let's discuss a few practical matters concerning spiritual Bible reading.

1. Find the time to read the Bible and be with God.

Theonas of Alexandria writes, "Let no day pass by without reading some portion of the Sacred Scriptures and giving some space to meditation; for nothing feeds the soul as well as those sacred studies do."[22]

We are busy, busy people. We race through the day. But I doubt that any of us would say we are busier than Jesus was when he walked the earth. Amid Jesus' busy schedule, he found time to be with the Father.

Mark 1:35 reads, "Very early in the morning, while it was still dark, Jesus got up, left the house and went off to a solitary place, where he prayed."

Most of us know the story of Jesus and his circle of three in the Garden of Gethsemane in Mark 14:32–41. Notice the difference between Jesus and his three disciples. Jesus is awake. Jesus is connecting with the Father. Too often, when we should be awake, we sleep. Let's not sleep through our Bible study. Let's wake up and begin the day with God.

If we understand the importance of study, then why do we not study as we should? Perhaps because study can be hard work. Bible study is a spiritual discipline, therefore it takes discipline. R.C. Sproul writes:

> Here then, is the real problem of our negligence. We fail to study God's word not so much because it is difficult to understand, not so much because it is dull and boring, but because it is work. Our problem is not a lack of intelligence or a lack of passion. Our problem is that we are lazy.[23]

Don't let laziness keep you from the Word. You can learn from God every day. Decide to spend some time in God's word daily. Over time, the reading of his word will change your life.

---

22. Theonas of Alexandria, c. 300, from *The Epistles of Theonas*, in the public domain.
23. R. C. Sproul, *Knowing Scripture* (Downers Grove: Intervarsity Press, 1997).

2. Read slowly.

Slow down. Savor each word. Ruminate. Ruminating is what a cow does when it chews the cud. Did you know that a cow has four stomachs? The first stomach is the rumen. When a cow grazes in the field, it swallows the grass, which sits for a while in the rumen. Then the cow regurgitates the cud and chews it some more. That's ruminating. When you read the Bible to feed your spirit, you ruminate on Scripture.

Reading the Bible is like eating your favorite dessert. When you eat your favorite dessert, you don't race through it. You savor every bite. I don't know what my favorite dessert is. I'm from the South, so I love Southern desserts. I love lemon ice box pie, my grandmother made an overwhelmingly awesome coconut cake, and Leigh's grandmother made an amazing chocolate pie. Its ingredients were butter, chocolate, and sugar; and then more butter, chocolate, and sugar.

When you bit into that pie, all your taste buds were on high alert. You'd bite into it and then you'd let it melt on your tongue. You'd start to hum, "Uhm. Uhm. Uhm." Then you'd swallow and say, "That's good pie!" You'd slowly cut another piece with your fork, lift it to your mouth, and place it on your tongue. That pie was so good that you wanted to slap somebody.

Sometimes we spend more time savoring a dessert than we do savoring the Bible. Psalm 119:103 reads, "How sweet are your words to my taste, sweeter than honey to my mouth!" Savor the Scriptures. Savor each bite of God's word.

3. Be an empty cup.

When we come to the Word, we need to make sure that our cup is empty. We need to be teachable. God says, "You will seek me and find me when you seek me with all your heart" (Jeremiah 29:13).

In Japan, a valued part of their culture is the tea ceremony. When you have a tea ceremony, it is important to follow proper protocol.

A successful businessman went to a tea master to learn the proper way to conduct a tea ceremony. He entered the master's house filled with pride, self-assurance, and disrespect. The tea master said nothing. He simply began the ceremony. When it came time to pour the tea, the tea master began to pour tea into the cup in front of the businessman. He poured the tea until it overflowed from the cup and ran onto the businessman's expensive suit.

The businessman rose from the floor in anger, shouting curses at the tea master. He asked, "What are you doing? I paid you good money to teach me this ceremony, and now you overfill my cup and ruin my suit." The tea master answered, "I can only teach you when your cup is empty. When your cup is full, I can teach you nothing." When we come to the Word, we need to make sure that we come with an empty cup.

4. Memorize.

In Psalm 119:11 the psalmist writes, "I have hidden your word in my heart that I might not sin against you."

When we put the word in our hearts, it helps keep sin out of our lives. Scriptures can be used as positive affirmation. Affirmations are like nitro fuel for the soul.

5. Avoid these two pitfalls.

A. Distractions – television, radio, negative people, the phone

B. Procrastination – I remember reading a story in a book entitled QBQ! The Question Before the Question,[24] in which the author related a time when he had a large piece of plate glass tilted against the basketball goal in front of his house. He knew it was a hazard, and he thought about moving it and properly disposing of the hazard. Instead, he procrastinated. Later in the evening, his wife asked their son to take out the trash. The author heard a loud crash come from the front of the house. In his heart, he knew exactly what had happened. His son must have walked into the plate glass. The father ran out the front door toward the basketball goal. Sure enough, his son had walked into the plate glass, smashing it to bits. Fortunately, his son escaped without harm. He didn't even have a scratch on him. But for the author, the lesson of procrastination was learned. When we procrastinate in our spiritual Bible reading, we are waiting for a spiritual crash. It will come. It's just a matter of when.

---

24. John G. Miller, *QBQ! The Question Behind the Question: Practicing Personal Accountability in Work and in Life* (New York: G.P. Putnam's Sons, 2012).

Rules for Reading[25]

Some of these practical points are repetitive. They were in the earlier list. However, as we have learned, repetition isn't bad. Perhaps by repeating a few points, they will sink deeper into our psyche.

1. Read the Bible daily.
2. Read the text repeatedly. G. Campbell Morgan read the book he was going to focus on fifty times before he wrote or preached on it. If it is a short letter, read it in one sitting. This is probably how it was read to the early disciples.
3. Read the Bible thoughtfully.
4. Read it patiently. Don't quit. Keep at it.
5. Read it selectively. Ask questions of the text:
   - Who? Who wrote it? Who are the main personalities?
   - What? What truths, events, substance, context?
   - When? What day, what year, what king, what era, what covenant?
   - Why? Why here? Why now? Why mention this?
   - Where? What location?
   - Wherefore? What difference does it make?
   - How? How am I going to apply this to my life?
6. Read prayerfully.
7. Read reflectively.
8. Read purposefully. Read with purpose. The Bible was written to equip us for every good work. Read with a desire to apply what you are reading to your life in order to help other people. The Bible transforms our lives so that we can help others.
9. Read spiritually. Don't get so bogged down in the facts and details that you miss the message of the text. Ask, "God, what do you want me to learn from this reading?" Pray, "God, speak. Your servant is listening."

---

25. I borrowed some of this material from a video teaching series by Dr. Mark Bailey of Dallas Theological Seminary as found on iTunes U, Dr. Mark Bailey BE101-02-02 and Dr. Mark Bailey BE101-02-03.

Underlining and Taking Notes

When you underline as you read, you focus more attention on the text. Studies show that you retain more from the text when you read with a pencil or pen in hand. You don't even have to use the pen, just holding it in your hand helps you retain more from the text. When you use the pen to underscore important points, the rate of retention heightens.

Mortimer Adler writes, "Reading a book should be a conversation between you and the author... Marking a book is literally an expression of your difference or your agreements with the author. It is the highest respect you can pay him."[26]

Adler and Van Doren list various devices that can be used when marking a passage.[27] I've added a few of my own to their list.

1. Underline major, important, or forceful statements.

2. Add vertical lines in the margins to emphasize an underlined statement or to point to a passage too long to underline.

3. Place a star, an asterisk, or a personal doodad in the margin to represent a very important idea. These should be used sparingly.

4. When you come across a sequence, place numbers in the margin or in the text to mark the sequence.

5. Circle key words, key phrases, or important ideas.

6. If you have a question you wish to ponder, place a question mark in the margin.

7. If there is a statement you wish to quote or memorize, write Q or M in the margin.

The important point is for you to find a system that works for you. When you mark up a text, you make it your own.

---

26. Adler, 49.
27. Adler, 49-51.

I love to see worn-out, marked-up Bibles. When I see pages that are yellow from the oil of the reader's hands, I know that Bible has been loved. Love your Bible. Treat it with respect, but wear it out with use. Treat it like a beloved friend. Have daily conversations with it. Take it out for coffee. Carry it with you wherever you go. The Bible was written to be read. In it are the words of life. As Fenelon said, "It is the source of truth." And as Michael W. Smith sings in the beautiful song "Ancient Words," its words were preserved for us for our walk in this world; they resound with God's own heart and will change us and guide us home if we let them impart his love and wisdom to us.[28]

Resources

Mortimer J. Adler and Charles Van Doren, *How to Read a Book* (New York, NY: Simon & Schuster, 2011).

Daniel Doriani, *Getting the Message: A Plan for Interpreting and Applying the Bible* (Phillipsburg, NY: P&R, 1996).

Gordon Fee, *How to Read the Bible Book by Book: A Guided Tour* (Grand Rapids, MN: Zondervan, 2009).

Gordon Fee and Douglas Stuart, *How to Read the Bible for All Its Worth* (Grand Rapids, MN: Zondervan, 2014).

G. Steve Kinnard, *Getting the Most from the Bible* (Spring, TX: Illumination, 2014).

William W. Klein, Craig L. Blomberg, and Robert L. Hubbard, Jr., *Introduction to Biblical Interpretation*.

M. Robert Mulholland Jr., *Shaped by the Word*.

T. Norton Sterrett, *How to Understand Your Bible*.

---

28. From www.sing365.com/music/lyric.nsf/Ancient-Words-lyrics-Michael-W-Smith.

CHAPTER THREE

Rhythms of the Sabbath and Solitude

Joel Peed, MA

Joel Peed has his MA in biblical studies and has served in the ministry for nearly thirty years. He and his wife, Christy, have been married for twenty-five years. With the recent adoption of their grandniece, they now have four children, three of whom are strong disciples. In 2017 Joel began the North American Small Church Committee, which has hosted two small church leadership conferences. In 2021 Joel was also asked to chair the ICOC Minister Health Task Force and has coached numerous ministers and congregations into a healthy ministerial sabbatical process. Joel and Christy have recently launched Waters of Rest Ministry (www.watersofrestministry.org), which aims to renew ministry families and the churches they serve through providing research, resources, and relationships to ministry staff around the world.

"Come to me, all you who are weary and burdened, and I will give you rest." (Matthew 11:28)

He makes me lie down in green pastures,
he leads me beside quiet waters,
he refreshes my soul. (Psalm 23:2–3)

You have made us for yourself, O Lord, and our heart is restless until it rests in you. —St. Augustine

Our world is in desperate need of rest for its soul. We live in an age of restless anxiety the likes of which have never been seen. Have the developments in psychology, technology, science, and research helped this epidemic of angst? Our ever-worsening statistics of depression and anxiety-related illnesses, physical and mental, would suggest the opposite. I would argue that the advancement of technology, in particular the smartphone and social media, have served to create a nonstop, hurried, and "nonpresent" existence that is crushing our collective soul. Into this restless darkness the living Christ speaks an invitation: "Come to me, all you who are weary and burdened...and you will find rest for your souls" (Matthew 11:28–29).

This invitation to rest didn't start with Jesus, but with the first example of sabbath in Genesis 2. Here we find, after six rhythmic (evening, morning...day 1) days of good work, God intentionally and emphatically brought his work to a close, carving out a day to cease and celebrate. This seventh day he both blessed and declared sacred, thus establishing a weekly rhythm of good work and good rest.

In the book of Exodus, we see this "God who rested" revealed personally as YHWH. In contrast to YHWH, Pharoah's anxiety had filled his being, motivated his leadership, and structured their culture. This anxious center led to a nonstop, never-enough, violent commoditizing of neighbor. Sound familiar? People weren't treated as humans, but as slaves valued only for what they could produce. Beneath this inhumane system, though, they were still human.

What does the soul do when it is neglected? How does it behave when its need for a sustainable rhythm of work and rest is marginalized, minimized, or accused as "lazy" by harsh taskmasters? Both an individual's and a community's collective soul cries out in desperation to its Creator! YHWH heard, and he hears today. Into the anxious, restless, and abusive system, YHWH compassionately (to the Israelite), and forcefully (to the Egyptian) intervened. He rescued his people not only from Pharoah, but from the whole anxious, restless, abusive system!

Even before the Mosaic law, YHWH provided water, food, and sabbath (Exodus 16). Then, in the Ten Commandments (Exodus 20; Deuteronomy 5), he invited the people to honor and remember the sabbath for two reasons. First, in the Exodus decalogue, he invites to sabbath because he himself practiced a work-

and-rest rhythm in Genesis 1 and 2. Second, in the Deuteronomy decalogue, he invites to sabbath to remind them of their redemption from the restless enslavement to an anxious Pharoah and his violent system. Therefore, the sabbath reminded them that they were free from the never-ending, commodity-driven god of productivity. Not only freedom *from*, but freedom *to* enter and enjoy the peaceful, covenant-centered YHWH, who delighted in them for who they were, not what they produced. The creator of the human soul and the creator of the historic sabbath are one. He knows what an anxious, weary, and burdened humanity needs: a sabbath rest for the soul, found ultimately in the Lord of the sabbath, Jesus Christ. Hallelujah, what a Savior!

Of course, with all created, pure, and beautiful gifts of God, spiritual forces of evil relentlessly twist his gifts into something dark, thus stealing their blessing. This is exactly what we see with the spiritual gift of sabbath. Over the centuries, anxiety and religion surrounded it, conforming sabbath into a legalistic performance to again earn the approval and satisfaction of God instead of communicating his approval (Isaiah 56:2) and satisfaction in his people. This time it was Jesus who intervened as the Lord of the sabbath and fulfilled its original intent as a gift of peace from a God at peace.

While it can appear that Jesus is anti-sabbath, a closer study reveals that he NEVER condemns the sabbath itself but does condemn the legalism surrounding it by some of the Jews. "The sabbath was made for man, not man for the sabbath" (Mark 2:27). Along with other legalistic practices, Jesus seems to intend to restore the sabbath to its original intent found in the Creator and his creation, not the Mosaic law and its subsequent anxious law keeping. Jesus restored the heart of the sabbath as a gift, created by God, mercifully given to humanity, to be received with gratitude. The sabbath was not intended to be a divisive identity marker performed by the super-spiritual as a measuring stick of righteousness and earned approval! It was intended to be a unifying (Isaiah 56), compassionate gift that would deeply meet a need of the human soul. Of course, we understand that Jesus himself was the ultimate fulfillment of the sabbath, along with the rest of the law. Therefore, the point is not sabbath keeping, but the eternal rest found in Christ alone.

But once again, this truth does not nullify the soul's need for rhythmic rest. Therefore, sabbath practice can serve as both a sign-post and a pathway to enter the eternal rest of Christ. The Apostle Paul specifically communicates that the gospel frees us from legalistic, judgmental, and identity-marking sabbath keeping, which further emphasizes the sabbath as a gift to be a burden-relieving, not a burden-producing, religious practice.

Fast-forward to today. Could this ancient practice still be relevant? Useful? Needed? A million times yes! God's invitation still stands, but why don't we receive it? Too busy? Too ashamed? Too anxious? Too guilty? Too tired? If there is even a hint of yes to those questions, you just qualified yourself as a prime candidate. While free of its legalistic requirements, the invitation to sabbath still provides YHWH's rescue from, and resistance to, the nonstop and ever-deepening restlessness we find in our culture, church, and collective soul. I have personally witnessed my soul, marriage, family, and church family being nourished and transformed through this spiritual discipline.

My wife and I have spent about twenty-five years experimenting with sabbatic rhythms in our spirituality, marriage, family life, and church life. We are enjoying its fruits and just can't keep it to ourselves! Here are a few tips we've learned along the way on how to fully receive and enjoy the blessings of sabbath.

Cease

- The word *shabbat* literally means "CEASE!" (emphasis God's, not mine!). One must carve out time to simply stop work (paid and unpaid), business, and busyness. Tradition has it that the Jews would have a "sabbath box" into which they would put something symbolic that represented their burden and work. As a minister, my sabbath typically begins on Sunday afternoon. My "sabbath box" is turning off my phone, and I can feel my soul experience instant relief!

- As our family gathers and enters our collective sabbath time, we often go for a walk or bike ride during the summer months to enjoy the evening calm and peace.

Celebrate

- We love food! One of the ways we celebrate is through enjoying good food together. Sometimes another family is included, but we make sure to emphasize that this is a time to celebrate together (all ministry chatter is off limits). We have a special "family fun" line item in our budget, which enables us to go to our favorite restaurant or order out pizza. Don't forget the garlic butter dipping sauce!

- We almost always find something to celebrate, from something monumental like adopting a fourth child, to simply a way we've seen God move this past week in or around us, to something light and fun like a certain child's accomplishment, or even Dad once again schooling the family in Wordle! The emphasis, though, is always brought back to celebrating who God is and his love and faithfulness to us (Psalm 92).

- We then move into some family fun: a board game, sporting event, favorite sitcom, or card game. Encouragement, competition, light (usually!) sarcasm, laughter, and good music are typically a part of the celebration.

Rest

- I then head off to our cabin on a lake that we inherited. Phone is off, clocks are unplugged, and so I sleep as long as my body needs. Even in waking, I have no agenda, so the sweet slow wake and half-dreamy state is nurtured.

- If I do get tired during the day, I immediately take a nap. It is amazing how replenished my mind, body, emotions, and soul feel after a day of physical rest. We cannot separate the spiritual from the physical, and our physical weariness will bear its fruit in clear unspirituality!

- Alex Pang wrote in his secular book entitled *Rest*,[29] "In the last couple decades discoveries in sleep research, psychology, neuroscience, organizational behavior, sports medicine, sociology, and other fields have given us a wealth of insight into the unsung but critical role that rest plays in strengthening the brain, enhancing learning, enabling inspiration, and making innovation sustainable."

- Most of us are far more exhausted than we realize, as we depend on caffeine and other adrenaline-producing stimulants to maintain energy. A chronic lack of sleep has body, mind, and soul consequences that will catch up with us. I am an "up early" type six days a week, so the seventh day gives my body what it needs to catch up. This rest's impact on my mental, emotional, and spiritual healing and overall health is unmistakable.

Contemplate

- This is my favorite part of my sabbath day—enjoying some solitude in nature to just be still and think. I grew up on a farm, and I still remember as a boy heading down to the pond in the springtime, sitting on the steel culvert, and simply pondering life. Now I sit with my coffee, enjoy God's beautiful creation, and think about:
  o Who is God? How is he revealing himself to me?
  o What is God's Spirit doing in me? Around me? In my family? In the church? In the world?
  o Who am I?
  o How am I feeling? Why?
  o What am I doing? Why?

- Of course, I read Scripture, but on this day the reading is different. I'm not preparing a lesson, I'm not thinking about the ministry (I ceased the afternoon before,

---

29. Alex Soojung-Kim Pang, *Rest: Why You Get More Done When You Work Less* (New York: Basic Books).

remember?), I'm just enjoying the Word as sweet honey from the honeycomb. The following I call my "comfort Scriptures" because sitting in them just makes me feel God's comfort: Isaiah 40–42; Psalm 92, 18, 23, 46; anything Jesus.

- As a natural people pleaser, human voices and feelings can ring loudly in my mind, producing a confusing static in my walk with God. Therefore, an unhurried space in time allows my mind the space to "spin out" enough to really listen to God. Often, I pray, "Speak, Lord, your servant is listening. What do you want me to hear? What do you want me to do? What do you want me to say? I am yours; here I am; do with me what you will." Then, I just breathe, be still, be quiet, and listen.

- Going for a long walk also has a way of helping my mind "spin out" and settle in to some deeper and spiritual thinking.

Saint Augustine states, "You have made us for yourself, O Lord, and our heart is restless until it rests in you." Is your restless heart in need of soul rest? Are the forces of this anxious age seeping into and wearying your soul? Jesus' invitation still stands. God's gift is still available. Taste and see, you won't be disappointed!

Practicing the Festival of the Booths in the Backyard
Angela and Michael DeAquino,
Evangelist and WML, Denver Church of Christ

"Get whatever you want, it's Sukkot." Our children were wide-eyed and a bit shocked that Mom and Dad were no longer holding the line on sugar intake. Every aisle in the grocery store presented more and more opportunities for new treats. We were about to celebrate the festival of booths for the first time, a holiday we see in Scripture that God commanded his people to celebrate.

We filled our cart with all kinds of treats, paid, and headed back to our home, where we set up our tents in the backyard to spend the next couple of days camping outside.

The next two days were filled with music, food, fun, and games along with other families and their kids. We collected cardboard boxes of all shapes and sizes, and the children made mini temporary shelters, each decorated with scriptures with our theme anthem: "This world is not our home!" That is what this festival is all about—a reminder that this world is temporary. That our hearts should be set in heaven, our true home. To not get caught up in worldly treasures. We memorialized the Israelites in the desert, as sojourners who lived in tents. God was preparing a new home for them in the promised land.

Sleeping outside in tents, eating good food, dancing to music, playing games, celebrating the hope of heaven—all in community with family and friends. This was a rich and beautiful time, a time that our kids will never forget and hopefully will pass on to the next generation.

Traditions and celebrations were God's designed way for parents to impress on their children their love for him and his law. When we incorporate any sort of message with food, music, fun, and community—engaging all our senses—it is a lot easier to pass down our beliefs through the generations. That is why God commanded his people to celebrate these festivals.

God offers his people these appointed festivals in which they were to celebrate. The festival of shelters/booths (also known as Sukkot, in Hebrew) was the last festival of the year.

"Celebrate this as a festival to the LORD for seven days each year. This is to be a lasting ordinance for the generations to come; celebrate it in the seventh month. Live in temporary shelters for seven days: All native-born Israelites are to live in such shelters so your descendants will know that I had the Israelites live in temporary shelters when I brought them out of Egypt. I am the LORD your God." (Leviticus 23:41–43)

Was it worth the money we spent splurging on food? Was it worth sleeping on the uncomfortable ground feet away from our Sleep Number bed? It sure was! As the next fall approached, we told the kids that we were going to do it again. "Are we going to sleep outside in tents and get all the treats we want?" We replied, "Yep! It's Sukkot!"

Resources

Marva Dawn, Keeping the Sabbath Wholly: Ceasing, Resting, Embracing, Feasting (Grand Rapids, MI: Eerdmans, 1989).

Wayne Cordeiro, Leading on Empty: Refilling Your Tank and Renewing Your Passion (Minneapolis, MN: Bethany House, 2009).

Walter Brueggemann, Sabbath as Resistance: Saying No to the Culture of Now (Louisville, KY: Westminster John Knox, 2017).

Wayne Muller, Sabbath: Finding Rest, Renewal, and Delight in Our Busy Lives (New York, NY: Bantam, 2000).

Lynne M. Baab, Sabbath Keeping: Finding Freedom in the Rhythms of Rest (Downers Grove, IL: InterVarsity, 2005).

Ruth Haley Barton, Sacred Rhythms: Arranging Our Lives for Spiritual Transformation. (Downers Grove, IL: IVP, 2006).

Check out your local opportunities for retreat facilities.

A unique opportunity is a retreat facility created by Shane and Sara Engle of the Great Land Christian Church in Anchorage, Alaska. Go to: glccalaska.org and hit the "Spiritual Retreats" tab for more information.

CHAPTER FOUR

The Call of the Wild:
Exploring the Spirituality of Nature

Shane Engle, MA

Shane Engel can be found sauntering through the mountains of Alaska with his wife of twenty years, Sara. They have three children: Luke, Lily, and Zoe. Both currently serve in the ministry for the Great Land Christian Church and have a marketing business and manage Adventure Corps International (a 501(c)3). In 1999, they started serving the church together in the youth and family ministry and are passionate about helping young people and families build their faith in God and strengthen each other as they are built on Christ. They have served in the ministry in New Jersey, New York, California, and Alaska. They both attended Rutgers University, where they met. Shane also has completed a master's in nonprofit leadership and management at the University of San Diego. The Engels manage the Gateway to the Arctic retreat facility near Talkeetna (about two hours north of Anchorage). For more information, go to www.glccalaska. org and hit the "Spiritual Retreats" tab.

There is an unbroken relationship between spirituality and nature. I used to tell people that I did not go to church growing up, as I grew up in a small farming town in Northwest New Jersey. Believe it or not, my New Jersey childhood consisted mainly of exploring the woods, fishing in creeks, tracking wildlife, and hiking the Appalachian Trail.

After looking back on my childhood and knowing what I now know about how God uses nature, I see that I was attending a communion service every time I entered the sanctuary of the wild. Every time I crossed the threshold of a tiny creek next to my house, I would be exposing myself to God's natural beauty and glory, which was filled with thousands of sermons that whispered to and calmed my heart. It was in this mystical land of what we called "the woods" where I would be called to learn and understand my Father. There was no need for a looking glass or a rabbit hole, as new worlds emerged after every fork in the trail.

> *The earth is the LORD's, and all it contains,*
> *The world, and those who dwell in it.*
> *For he has founded it upon the seas*
> *And established it upon the rivers. (Psalm 24:1–2 NASB 1995)*

> *But ask the animals, and they will teach you,*
> *or the birds in the sky, and they will tell you;*
> *or speak to the earth, and it will teach you*
> *or let the fish in the sea inform you.*
> *Which of all these does not know*
> *that the hand of the LORD has done this?*
> *In his hand is the life of every creature*
> *and the breath of all mankind. (Job 12:7–10)*

> *Let the heavens rejoice, let the earth be glad;*
> *let the sea resound, and all that is in it.*
> *Let the fields be jubilant, and everything in them*
> *let all the trees of the forest sing for joy. (Psalm 96:11–12)*

> *In his hand are the depths of the earth,*
> *and the mountain peaks belong to him.*
> *The sea is his, for he made it,*
> *and his hands formed the dry land. (Psalm 95:4–5)*

The trees clapped, the birds rejoiced, and branches were arms outstretched toward the heavenly realms. I sensed his presence early on in these sacred places and have often referred to these places and times as home. I found the wilderness to be a sanctuary during the tumultuous times of life, as the natural places were places where I was fully seen, fully myself, and felt deeply connected (to what?).

Many times, I would wander off, and each wandering felt like an adventure. I discovered new trails, each offering its rewards: a lily pad-covered pond, a darkened cave, and plenty of mountain summits. Surely God was in the midst. He was planting seeds of faith deeply into my soul as a witness to his marvelous creation.

Despite my background and over twenty years of ministry, only recently have I seriously studied the Scriptures to learn how God uses nature to help us humans understand his character and glimpse his power. The irony of my story is that I was in one of the most beautiful cities in the world, San Diego. Yet despite its ninety miles of beaches, my soul was longing for the deep woods, untamed rivers, and revelations that lay hidden in the backcountry. It was the realization that I personally needed a stronger and deeper connection with nature so that I could nurture my relationship with God.

My family made the bold leap of faith to move to Alaska after we had discussed that it was important for us to be closer to nature. As God would have it, he put us in the most spectacular place; it was soon thereafter that an opportunity presented itself to serve in the ministry in Alaska. God surely heard my prayer.

Being in Alaska has afforded me the opportunity not only to study the Scriptures in a deeper manner but also to experience his nature in ways that only Alaska can provide. I have been able to fly around the summit of Denali and then sleep in its shadow, traverse glaciers, sit in meadows, fish the elusive king salmon, hand-feed bald eagles, be stalked by bears, chase wild moose through downtown Anchorage and ultimately stand in awe of the sheer majesty and grandeur in his creation. As a result of what I learned from Scripture and what I have experienced in the backcountry, I have become more and more convinced of our need to be connected to God through his creation. Scripture, again and again, emphasizes the opportunity to look at nature and see God.

Seeing God use nature and seeing God in nature are both examples of what has been coined as the "spirituality of nature." There are many ways to view and understand God in this manner, and the hope of this essay is simply to spark or deepen a desire to connect with God and his Spirit in and through nature. Additionally, you do not need to move to Alaska to appreciate how God uses nature. Many urban areas offer spaces where you could get a glimpse into God. One can appreciate a small flower on the windowsill in an apartment on the fifteenth floor of a high-rise. Regardless of your location, I believe that we all have the capability to see God in refreshing ways by interacting with his creation.

The classic scripture that many people turn to for understanding the spirituality of nature is Romans 1:20:

> *For since the creation of the world His invisible attributes, His eternal power and divine nature, have been clearly seen, being understood through what has been made, so that they are without excuse.* (NASB1995)

The book of Romans clearly states that his creation is a primary source of instruction, inspiration, and insight into who he is and how we should live. The Holy Spirit is so confident in nature's ability to reveal God's power and nature that he says it leaves all without excuse! This alone reveals to us that there is an unbroken relationship between God and nature. One can simply investigate what God has created and come to a greater understanding of his holiness, goodness, beauty, and majesty. (There is much to be said about the Christian's role in being good stewards of God's earth and the impact our societies have had on our environment; however, we will save that for another time.)

In our often hurried and busy lives, we can overlook the ways that nature teaches us about God. It's not uncommon to hear people say they want to spend more time in nature but for one reason or another just cannot make it out of their bustling neighborhoods. However, in a holistic view of spirituality, it is difficult to deny the importance of spending time with God in nature. Researchers and scientists are constantly affirming the health benefits of nature, stating that exposure to nature not only makes us feel better emotionally,[30] it contributes to our physical well-being, reducing blood pressure, heart rate, muscle tension, and

---

30. https://e360.yale.edu/features/ecopsychology-how-immersion-in-nature-benefits-your-health

the production of stress hormones.[31] It may even reduce mortality, according to scientists such as public health researchers Stamatakis and Mitchell.[32]

If we turn our eye to the Gospels and look at Jesus' relationship with nature, I believe that we will be inspired further to be like him, not just in word but in his practices. Many times, Jesus' teachings are lessons learned from what could be observed by spending time in nature. The images Jesus conveys are for the most part from the natural world, although he never once uses the word "nature." He uses lessons learned from fig trees, soil, fish, water, sheep, goats, lambs, thunderstorms, wheat, weeds, vineyards, waves, and more! His teachings about the kingdom of heaven are oriented toward the understanding that the kingdom is like a mountain.

"Consider how the wildflowers grow," Jesus instructed. "They do not labor or spin. Yet I tell you, not even Solomon in all his splendor was dressed like one of these. If that is how God clothes the grass of the field, which is here today, and tomorrow is thrown into the fire, how much more will he clothe you—you of little faith!" (Luke 12:27) We all can benefit from the exhortation to consider the lilies.

It is also important to note how Jesus exampled his time on earth. Jesus spent most of his time outdoors and reflected upon the natural order so that we could understand him and the way he wants us to live. Scriptures describe Jesus often retreating to the wilderness, practicing solitude, and ascending to the mountains to pray. This fact is important. His is a practice worthy of imitation.

Furthermore, it is estimated that Jesus walked over 900 miles during his short three-year ministry tenure. This afforded plenty of time to reflect, pray, and contemplate what the Spirit wanted him to convey to his people. For a long time, we have taught people to pray using the Lord's prayer along with an acronym to further understand its structure. But we can teach not only the intellectual construct of the Lord's prayer but also the where and how Jesus

31. https://www.mind.org.uk/information-support/tips-for-everyday-living/nature-and-mental-health/how-nature-benefits-mental-health
32. https://www.sciencedirect.com/science/article/pii/S0169204611003665

prayed. Our best encouragement can be as simple as to go to the mountains. Go to the river. Go to the valley. Go outside and pray. Inadvertently, we can cultivate a culture of indoor Christians, whereas I see Jesus predominantly living his prayer life outdoors.

The most famous of his sermons take place in the mountains. Jesus often withdrew to the wilderness to pray alone or with his disciples. It was in the mountains that he appointed the twelve apostles, and it was on a mountain that the transfiguration took place. It seems that his favorite place to withdraw and pray was outdoors on the Mount of Olives, where he often sat, prayed, and cried. What is interesting about this is that this was outside the walls of the city, not far from the temple. It raises the question, why go to the mountains and not into the temple? This curious question has led me to one of the biggest scriptural revelations that has shaped my life thus far.

Throughout biblical history, God uses the wilderness and sacred outside places to reveal himself to "the called" and to prepare them for service and leadership! Despite having the tabernacle, the tent of meeting, and eventually the temple, God chooses to reveal himself to his leaders in and through nature. He does not reveal himself through the "official offices" God had them design and construct.

The list is astounding. Adam and Eve were placed in a garden instead of an already constructed temple of worship. God chose to reveal himself to Abraham through the splendor of the stars and the deliverance of his son through a wild stag, in the thicket. Moses was called by God through a burning bush outside, instead of God revealing himself inside the palace. Noah's deliverance was through the profound display of natural elements and animals. Jacob wrestled God outside, Elijah was spoken to on the edge of a mountain, and furthermore, was refreshed by ravens under a broom tree. Jonah was swallowed by a large fish. Hagar fled to the wilderness...and the list goes on and on. We also must take note that God sends Israel into the wilderness for forty years! Why is this so?

According to *The Brown-Driver-Briggs Hebrew and English*

Lexicon, the Hebrew word for wilderness is *midbar* (רבדמ). *Midbar,* as you would expect, means wilderness or desert, but surprisingly, it is also the word for an organ of speech. In other words, the wilderness is God's mouthpiece or his organ of speech! God uses nature to speak to his people!

> The heavens declare the glory of God;
>   the skies proclaim the work of his hands.
> Day after day they pour forth speech;
>   night after night they reveal knowledge.
> They have no speech, they use no words;
>   no sound is heard from them.
> Yet their voice goes out into all the earth,
>   their words to the ends of the world. (Psalm 19:1–4)

> "Therefore I am now going to allure her;
>   I will lead her into the wilderness
>   and speak tenderly to her.
> There I will give her back her vineyards,
>   and will make the Valley of Achor door of hope." **(Hosea 2:14–15)**

Convention would lead us to believe that wilderness is both challenging terrain (desert) and a metaphor for a challenging time in life. Israel wandered for forty years in the wilderness as a punishment. However, if we dig deeper, it can be clearly seen that God uses the wilderness to speak to his people and train them for victories in the future. This idea of the wilderness as God's mouthpiece, coupled with Jesus' example and relationship with the wilderness, leads me to strongly believe that we should actively seek the wilderness. This is a spiritual act of seeking God for intervention in our lives. Psalm 121 asks a poignant question: When I lift up my eyes to hills, where does my help come from? The answer? My help comes from the Maker of heaven and earth! When we lift up our eyes to the hills, God revives us and strengthens us. Many of my formative moments with God, much like the biblical evidence we looked at, happen in nature.

Most notably, God has used the wilderness to help me on a personal level in my most difficult times of grief, conflict, and insecurity. When I go out into the wilderness and connect with God, it is a game changer for me. It's a reminder of how powerful God is and how small I am. My mind slows down, and I can reconnect with God, but I also reconnect with myself. Parker Palmer[33] in his book *A Hidden Wholeness: The Journey Toward an Undivided Life* speaks to how wilderness helps us connect with ourselves and describes our souls like wild animals:

> Like a wild animal, the soul is tough, resilient, resourceful, savvy, and self-sufficient: it knows how to survive in hard places. Yet despite its toughness, the soul is also shy. Just like a wild animal, it seeks safety in the dense underbrush, especially when other people are around. If we want to see a wild animal, we know that the last thing we should do is go crashing through the woods yelling for it to come out. But if we will walk quietly into the woods, sit patiently at the base of a tree, breathe with the earth, and fade into our surroundings, the wild creature we seek might put in an appearance. We may see it only briefly and only out of the corner of an eye—but the sight is a gift we will always treasure as an end in itself.

The glimpses of the soul supplied by God in the natural world provide counsel and add depth to my spiritual journey like no other activity. God's heart is revealed in nature.

In closing, I would like to offer John Muir's thoughts on how we should interact with nature and the wilderness. John Muir[34] hated the word "hiking" and encouraged people to use the word "sauntering" instead. A long time ago during the Middle Ages, people used to make a pilgrimage to the Holy Land. When people asked the adventurer where they were going, they responded, "A la

---

32. Parker J. Palmer is a world-renowned writer, speaker, and activist who focuses on issues in education, community, leadership, spirituality, and social change. He has reached millions worldwide through his nine books, including *Let Your Life Speak, The Courage to Teach, A Hidden Wholeness,* and *Healing the Heart of Democracy.*

34. John Muir was perhaps this country's most famous and influential naturalist. He was also involved in the creation of Yosemite National Park and Grand Canyon, Kings Canyon, Petrified Forest, and Mt. Rainier National Parks.

Sainte Terre"—which means to the Holy Land. So these pilgrims were later described as "Sainte-Terre-ers," which later became those who saunter.

The wild spaces that God provides to you, whether in the backcountry of Alaska or in the downtown beauty of Central Park, ought to be "sauntered" through. We can and should approach our wilderness experiences reverently, not just crash through the woods and spook all the wildlife. Wandering through nature is a contemplative exercise of sauntering, drawing us into nature as a sacred place.

We are invited to wander, or saunter, until a place or being that feels both alluring and dangerous "calls to us." This is the call of the wild. It is a contemplative practice. Sauntering happens without rushing, allowing you to deeply pay attention and listen to the woodland creature called your soul. This is an invitation to depart from the familiar and step into what is wild and unknown.

CHAPTER FIVE

Practicing Meditation:
Filling the Well

Dr. Tracy Jones, EdD

Dr. Tracy Jones is a member of the Boston Church of Christ and has been a disciple since 1996. She is married and has four children. She received a master's in counseling psychology from Lesley University and a doctoral degree in the field of Christian counseling from Liberty University. Her research has been in using Christian meditation to treat anxiety, depression, and shame. She has been a clinician since 1997 and is a member of the executive management team at CrossPoint Clinical Services, a faith-based counseling and wellness nonprofit. Tracy enjoys hiking, cheering on her kids in their various endeavors, traveling, reading, and drinking tea. She has a passion for helping people see God's love and listen to his Spirit by learning to be quiet in his presence. Her favorite scripture is Exodus 14:14: "The Lord will fight for you, you need only to be still."

Tracy Jones, EdD, LPC, LMHC, CMIP — www.crosspointclinical.org
Instagram: @dr.tracyjones; linkedin.com/in/drtracyjones

We not only read and hear and inquire, but we meditate on what comes before us; that is, we withdraw into silence where we prayerfully and steadily focus upon it. In this way its meaning for us can emerge and form us as God works in the depths of our heart, mind, and soul. —Dallas Willard, *Spirit of the Disciplines*[35]

In the same way that the word of a person who is dear to me follows me throughout the day, so the Word of Scripture should resonate and work within

---

35. Dallas Willard, *The Spirit of the Disciplines* (United Kingdom: HarperCollins, 1990),177.

me ceaselessly. Just as you would not dissect and analyze the word spoken by someone dear to you, but would accept it just as it was said, so you should accept the Word of Scripture and ponder it in your heart as Mary did. That is all. That is meditation.   —Dietrich Bonhoeffer, *Meditating on the Word* [36]

Have you ever wondered what meditation is or if it is righteous for a Christian to meditate? I have often encountered resistance to meditation, with fellow Christians or people I see in my counseling practice telling me they are afraid it is going to be "a hippy thing," "a New Age idea," or that it will make them focus on themselves and lose sight of God. So let me start by reassuring you, we could develop an entire practice of daily meditation without ever leaving the pages of the Bible! It is a practice commanded by God that has deep, life-changing benefits for our contentment, our replenishment, our obedience, our surrender, and our intimacy with God.

Many traditions and religions have utilized the discipline of meditation since ancient times and have recognized the power of this tool to focus the heart and mind. Modern-day Christians, however, are often unfamiliar with this practice and fear the Buddhist connotations it has developed in popular culture and the mainstream mindfulness found in various media. While the goal of some forms of meditation is detachment, an emptying of the mind, or a focus on the self as central, in Christian meditation the express purpose is attachment to the Creator, a filling of the mind with the word, character, or truths of God.

To achieve this profound union with God, we need to first disengage from the attachments of the world and then be intentional about what we put in its place. When I think of doing this, I am reminded of Luke 11:24–26, where Jesus says:

> *"When an impure spirit comes out of a person, it goes through arid places seeking rest and does not find it. Then it says, 'I will return to the house I left.' When it arrives, it finds the house swept clean and put in order. Then it goes and*

---

36. Dietrich Bonhoeffer, *Meditating on the Word* (Lanham, MD: Cowley, 2000), 22.

takes seven other spirits more wicked than itself, and they go in and live there. And the final condition of that person is worse than the first."

It is clear from this passage that for Christians, simply clearing the world out of our hearts and minds will not be enough; we also need to focus on filling the space with the attributes of God, or we risk a graver condition. This emptying and intentional filling can be achieved through meditation.

Although there is sometimes a fear that to meditate is to step outside the Christian faith and principles, Christianity in fact has a rich heritage of the use of meditation to connect with God.

Both the Hebrew and the Greek cultures had meditation practices that would have been familiar to the recipients of the Bible; therefore, Scripture uses several Hebrew and Greek words to describe meditation, and to meditate is mentioned over and over throughout Scripture. To give you a sample from Strong's Bible Dictionary:

In the Hebrew

- *suwach* meaning to meditate, muse, commune, speak, or contemplate – *Genesis 24:63*
- *siyach* meaning to put forth, meditate, muse, commune, speak, complain, ponder, sing, or consider – *Psalm 77:3, 6, 12; Psalm 119:15, 23, 27, 48, 78, 97, 148; Psalm 145:5*
- *hagah* meaning to moan, growl, utter, muse, mutter, meditate, groan, or imagine – *Joshua 1:8; Psalm 1:2; Psalm 63:6; Psalm 77:1; Isaiah 33:18*

In the Greek

- *meletaō* meaning to care for, meditate, attend to carefully, practice, or revolve in the mind – *Mark 13:11; 1 Timothy 4:15*
- *promeletáō* meaning to consider, ponder, or meditate beforehand – *Luke 21:14*

Meditation in the Bible is portrayed as a common activity that was done regularly by God's people. These times of quiet contemplation were often followed by increased understanding, peace, and blessings. Meditation is first mentioned in Genesis 24:63 as it talks about Isaac: "He went out to the field one evening to meditate, and as he looked up, he saw camels approaching." This was just before he met Rebekah, his future bride and blessing!

The vast majority of the mention of meditation in the Scriptures is in the form of an instruction for God's people regarding how to interact with his law. The Bible directs us to study, obey, teach to others, talk about, read, and meditate on the Scriptures; each of these being its own unique command.

Our brains are designed to gain increased perspective from every one of these activities, and we benefit from each in distinctive ways. We may not even have seen these as separate disciplines, as we often meld one into another, which is appropriate and good. For instance, we may read a passage of Scripture and then teach it to someone else while we are also focusing on obeying what it says.

Although it is important to notice that followers are commanded to meditate on the Scriptures, if we are unfamiliar with this practice, we may inadvertently pass over it or confuse it with something else. It is common for Christians to equate studying Scripture with meditating on it, but these practices have significant differences. It is more natural for me to study and "do" than it is for me to absorb, contemplate, and "be" with a scripture, and I suspect I am not alone in this.

We live in a fast-paced culture in which we are expected to produce and "do" constantly. Busy has become our shared language. Meditation may be a foreign concept, as it is a slowing down, being present to Scripture, and letting it tumble and unfold in our heart, not an intellectual gathering of information or an exercise in exegesis. Although we gain knowledge through study, there are many things in life that we cognitively understand but do not believe, practice, or live out. In fact, our understanding of many things helps us decide not to live from those concepts!

God calls us to plant Scripture in a place from which it can be lived and experienced. This is different from having an academic knowledge of the Scriptures. Meditation is the mechanism for moving a scripture or a characteristic of God from our brain to our heart so that we can live from it and experience the freedom and exhilaration of it and so that we can decide and speak and react from it. There is power in meditation; power to act, to focus, and to obey from a heart of acceptance, surrender, love, and peace.

The many actions of our faith are meant to work together to move us closer to God. To bypass meditation is to avoid an integral aspect of walking with God and ultimately to miss out on the fullness, richness, and depth offered in a relationship with him. In the book, *Knowing God*, J. I. Packer explains:

> Meditation is a lost art today, and Christian people suffer grievously from their ignorance of the practice. Meditation is the activity of calling to mind, and thinking over, and dwelling on, and applying to oneself the various things that one knows about the works and ways and purposes and promises of God. It is an activity of holy thought, consciously performed in the presence of God, under the eye of God, with the help of God, as a means of communion with God.[37]

In the Bible, meditation is not only commanded (Joshua 1:8), but commonplace, we could do it day and night (Psalms 39:3; 48:9; 77:3, 6, 12; 119:15), it brings blessings (Psalm 1:2), and it brings clarity and understanding while being pleasing to God (Psalms 19:14; 49:3; 104:34). Since it is a tool that plants the word of God in our inner being, it is not surprising that it is often followed by obedience (Joshua 1:8). Meditation is seen as a way to commune with God and to discern a course of action. When we meditate on the Word, we have our hearts and minds emptied of our own ways and filled with the ways of God, allowing the Holy Spirit to facilitate greater understanding of God and surrender to his ways. He gives us what we need to move forward. John 14:26 tells us, "The Advocate, the Holy Spirit, whom the Father will send in my

37. J. I. Packer, *Knowing God* (United Kingdom: InterVarsity Press, 2021), 23.

name, will teach you all things and will remind you of everything I have said to you." Meditation is a way to open yourself to the guidance of the Holy Spirit.

Scripture advises us to remember and meditate on God's law (Joshua 1:8; Psalms 1:2; 119:97), unfailing love (Psalm 48:9), mighty/wonderful deeds/works (Psalms 77:12; 119:27; 143:5; 145:5), precepts and ways (Psalm 119:15, 78), decrees and statutes (Psalm 119:2, 48, 99), and promises (Psalm 119:148). We are to meditate on God's character, his word, his actions, and his love for us because doing so equips us to live fully in his grace.

As Psalm 1:1–3 teaches us:

> *Blessed is the one*
> *who does not walk in step with the wicked*
> *or stand in the way that sinners take*
> *or sit in the company of mockers,*
> *but whose delight is in the law of the LORD,*
> *and who meditates on his law day and night.*
> *That person is like a tree planted by streams of water,*
> *which yields its fruit in season*
> *and whose leaf does not wither—*
> *whatever they do prospers.*

Meditation and Prayer

Meditation also has a deep impact on our prayer life. Remember, the actions of our faith are connected. Donald Whitney, in his book, *Spiritual Disciplines for the Christian Life*, explains:

> Here's the simple, but extraordinarily powerful truth: Meditation is the missing link between Bible intake and prayer. Too often disjointed, the two should be united.
>
> Typically, we read the Bible, close it, and then try to shift gears into prayer. But many times, it seems as if the gears between the two won't mesh. In fact, after some forward progress during our time in the Word, shifting to prayer sometimes feels like suddenly slipping back into neutral or even reverse. Instead, there should be a smooth, almost unnoticeable transition between

Scripture input and prayer output so that we move even closer to God in those moments. This happens when we insert the link of meditation in between.[38]

Reading the Bible tends to be a cognitive exercise and prayer a pouring out of our hearts to God. This is a big shift for our brain. Have you ever found that difficult? Have you had a tough time connecting emotionally to God in prayer after a great Bible study? Do you find one easier than the other? Meditation can provide the bridge for our brain to make this shift and connection fluently and effectively.

Meditation is a vehicle to transformation, increased understanding, insight, and healing. When we contemplate, ponder, and apply God's word, it moves from our cognitive realm to the core of who we are. Meditation helps us to love God with all our heart, mind, and strength. Romans 12:2 tells us, "Do not conform to the pattern of this world, but be transformed by the renewing of your mind. Then you will be able to test and approve what God's will is—his good, pleasing, and perfect will." Meditation on the Scriptures facilitates this transformation of our minds.

When I think of the power of meditation, I think of Peter walking on the water to Jesus. "Then Peter got down out of the boat, walked on the water, and came toward Jesus. But when he saw the wind, he was afraid and, beginning to sink, cried out, 'Lord, save me!'" (Matthew 14:29–30). What I love about this story is the water. Jesus did not do anything miraculous to the water itself. The miracle, in fact, was that he was walking on ordinary water. Peter was a fisherman. His whole life was on the water! He knew water and all its physical properties; he had probably jumped into and sunk in water every day. Yet when his focus and intention was fully on Jesus, all the things he knew about water did not matter.

Meditation works like this. It is not magical, and it will not change your environment or your situations. It will change you! It is a tool to get us focused on God and will therefore change our experience of these things. It teaches us how to fully trust and offers

---

38. D. S. Whitney, *Spiritual Disciplines for the Christian Life* (Colorado Springs, CO: NavPress, 2014), 86.

a way to keep our eyes fixed on God and not on the winds around us. It is a means of letting go of our intellectual explanations and solutions and opening ourselves to the supernatural power of God's Spirit.

> *Now the Lord is the Spirit, and where the Spirit of the Lord is, there is freedom. And we all, who with unveiled faces contemplate the Lord's glory, are being transformed into his image with ever-increasing glory, which comes from the Lord, who is the Spirit.* (2 Corinthians 3:17–18)

How to Meditate

So how do we meditate? To meditate is to dwell on a scripture carefully and deeply, to thoughtfully consider, to ponder, reflect on, prayerfully contemplate, call to mind, and picture God's word, store it in your heart, and claim the promises and character of God. It helps you to move forward with humility, focus, and intention.

In the Jewish tradition, meditation involves speaking a scripture over and over, and in the Greek tradition, it involves deeply contemplating the scripture. Both require making space and being willing to be filled by Scripture alone for that moment. It is a practice, meaning the more you practice it, the more benefit you receive.

The busier we are, the more we need it, and Jesus is our example of this. Luke 5:16 tells us "Jesus often withdrew to lonely places and prayed." This passage follows a description of the incredibly full healing and teaching schedule maintained by our Savior. In the midst of all the needs and demands, the deep compassion and care, Jesus regularly, often, withdrew from it all to be with God. This is what kept him fortified and able to give. He did not wait until there were no more needs or until his well had run dry. He seems to have known that the well would need to be continuously filled for him to be consistently serving and giving. That is a hard lesson for me and likely for you as well! How often do we give until we have nothing left or avoid giving altogether for fear we will be overdrawn? Daily, persistent meditation is a tool to ensure your well is always full, no matter what else is happening; and to notify you when your spiritual water level starts getting low.

Learning to meditate is like learning anything else—we need to practice regularly to build confidence. It is not a matter of gaining knowledge, and thankfully, it is not complicated. However, that does not mean it will come easy to us. We learn it by doing it. And we get better at it by doing it more.

Some suggestions to get started: It is helpful to find a quiet space, a space where you can be free from distractions and alone to meditate. It can be in your favorite chair, a closet in your house, out in nature, or even going for a quiet walk in your neighborhood.

Choose a consistent time and a place where you feel safe and comfortable; and give yourself grace as you are discovering what works for you. Try to free yourself from distractions as best you can. Our senses easily pull our focus away, so think about what sounds, smells, temperatures, or sensations may distract you. The visual field quickly gets the brain going in many directions, so often closing your eyes is helpful if you are able.

I propose starting with ten minutes per day. It may not seem like much time, but often when people are starting out, the mind will wander and easily lose focus, and suddenly ten minutes will feel like an hour! You will be thirty seconds in and already you are thinking about the meeting you have later or what you ate for breakfast. Just accept that this is part of the process of growing in this new skill and be gentle with yourself. You are training your brain to be quiet and unhurried and to be still and receptive. You are training yourself to "be" instead of "do": to not calculate, criticize, or figure out, but to receive. Meditation builds our relationship with God. Give yourself time to learn how to let him speak to you in this way.

Practice Meditation

Let's try a simple exercise in Scripture meditation. First take a moment to situate yourself somewhere you can be alone and uninterrupted. Choose a scripture or a portion of Scripture that can be said in the span of a breath or two. One of my favorites is Exodus 14:14: "The Lord will fight for you, you need only to be still."

Sit in a comfortable, upright position. Now either close your eyes or focus on a single point in front of you to decrease any visual distraction. Say a short prayer asking God to guide you in this time with him. Take a full minute to just be still and breathe, noticing but not trying to change your breath. Your breath is a reminder of God breathing his life into you. Breathe in and out naturally, comfortably; feeling the breath enter your nostrils and down into your belly. Notice your abdomen expanding and falling. The rhythm of your breath may become slower and fuller. Your body may become more relaxed. Just allow yourself to settle and breathe.

Now take a deep breath in and as you exhale say the scripture out loud. You can use two breaths to complete the scripture, saying half on one exhale and half on the next exhale, if you need to. Take another breath in, slower this time, and say the scripture as you slowly exhale. Repeat this breathing in and speaking the scripture slowly over and over.

If your mind wanders into other thoughts, know that this is normal; no need to criticize yourself. Gently release those thoughts into God's hands and bring your attention back to the scripture, breathing in and speaking the scripture again and again. Notice any thoughts or feelings that arise as the words pass through your mind and out your lips. Don't try to control or direct your breath or your thoughts or your feelings. Just be with the scripture. Let it rest on you, sit with you; be in you. Breathe in and say the scripture as you exhale. In with the breath and out with the scripture, over and over. Now allow your mind to just be still and quiet. Let it absorb the scripture as fully as you can for this moment. Simply breathe and be still. Notice any thoughts or feelings that are with you now.

Say a short prayer thanking God for this time together. As the meditation comes to an end, open your eyes and become aware of your surroundings.

What was this experience like for you? Peaceful? Uncomfortable? Were you surprised by how quickly your mind tried to go someplace else? Did it feel like your senses went into overdrive and each sensation pulled you away from your focus? Did you begin to settle down as you persisted? Did you connect to the scripture you had chosen in a new way or gain new insights?

I encourage you to do a Scripture meditation in the morning and then return to it with a simple breath in and exhaling out the scripture throughout the day. You take over 22,000 breaths each day, so just use a few throughout your day to allow yourself to return to this place of being with God through the scripture. Once you have practiced this, it will be easier for your brain to quickly return to this place as you breathe in and out throughout your day. Experiment with it.

Try meditating while lying prostrate, while walking, standing, kneeling, or sitting. Try with your arms raised in reverence or with your hands palms up on your lap, opened and ready to receive. If ten minutes felt impossible, try five. Start where you are at and build from there. Add a minute or two each week and see where it leads you. What would it be like if you meditated for an hour, a morning, a day? Try doing the same scripture for several days or a week or a month to see how your connection with it and understanding of it change.

Additional Meditation Ideas

You can also go into nature and meditate on God's artistry, his character displayed in what you see around you. Imagine and ponder his fingerprint on the moon or his voice in the rain. Use your other senses to meditate on the sounds, tastes, or smells of the beach, a forest, the birds as they sing. Meditate on the feel of the breeze or the sun on your face. Notice how you begin to see the Creator's love in the creation. Allow this to connect you to him. What does this do to your sense of awe? Do you begin to see yourself the way he sees you? How does this change how you worship him?

I pray that as you venture into the practice of meditation, your heart will be open and excited for the depths this can bring to your relationship with God. Remember it is an instrument to draw you closer to the heart, mind, and character of God. It is a way to access deeper realms in your partnership with him and to connect to his love.

In the words of Richard Foster in *Celebration of Discipline*,

"If you believe that we live in a universe created by the infinite-personal God who delights in our communion with him, you will see meditation as communication between the Lover and the one beloved."[39]

You are truly the beloved of God. Be creative as you learn to commune with him in this way and be gentle and graceful with yourself as you learn new skills. Enjoy the journey meditation provides into the profound mystery of God's infinite love for you personally and let his Spirit guide you as you more fully unite with him and his will for you. Allow him to fill your spiritual well!

Resources

D. Bonhoeffer, *Meditating on the Word* (United States: Cowley Publications, 2000).

R. J. Foster, *Celebration of Discipline: The Path to Spiritual Growth* (United Kingdom: HarperCollins, 1988).

J. I. Packer, *Knowing God* (United Kingdom: InterVarsity Press, 2021).

D. S. Whitney, *Spiritual Disciplines for the Christian Life* (United States: The Navigators, 2014).

D. Willard, *The Spirit of the Disciplines* (United Kingdom: HarperCollins, 1990).

---

39. Foster, *Celebration of Discipline*, 23.

CHAPTER SIX

Acceptance and Mindfulness

Dr. Jennifer Konzen, PsyD

Jennifer Konzen, PsyD, LMFT, CST, CCDC, is the director of the Center for Sexuality in San Diego, CA. She is a licensed marriage and family therapist, a certified sex therapist, and a certified chemical dependency counselor. She is also a two-time nationally award-winning researcher, an international speaker, an adjunct professor in San Diego at Bethel Seminary and Alliant International University and online at Rocky Mountain School of Ministry and Theology. Dr. Konzen is the author of *The Art of Intimate Marriage, Redeemed Sexuality,* and *The Ransomed Journey: Couples Recovery from Addiction.* She lives in San Diego, California, where she has been shepherding and leading in the marrieds ministry and the youth and family ministry.

Do you ever have thoughts that just keep whirring around in your head? Do you ever have emotional responses that you really wish you didn't have? Do you sometimes feel you get stuck in thinking or feeling a certain way and you feel a bit lost in how to feel or think differently? Are there ways your body responds to life or circumstances that trouble or frustrate you? Do you feel like you respond quickly to things that you go through, and you wish you could not react so strongly? Do you get pictures or images in your mind that you just wish weren't there? Do you have emotions you feel are sinful? Do you have thoughts or fears that you feel you shouldn't have? Do you keep trying to "take captive every thought" and it just isn't working?

As those who love God, we want to be able to live out this scripture: "May these words of my mouth and this meditation of my heart be pleasing in your sight, Lord, my Rock and my Redeemer"

(Psalm 19:14). We want to think and feel and respond like Jesus would, who said, "I always do what pleases him" (John 8:29). And God does promise to show us the path to get there, to have a heart that pleases him and to have thoughts and responses that reflect the Spirit he has put in us.

Sometimes, though, our thoughts and feelings and the sensations we get in our body (the quick heat to the face when we are angry, the drop in our stomach of fear, the tightness of the shoulders when we are anxious) come in all of a sudden or just don't seem to listen when we try to take them captive and direct them to a godly place. You may be having issues with stress, anxiety, depression, or discouragement. It can be difficult to know how to deal with these kinds of emotions or mental states. We often wonder how to take some of our problem emotions to God.

Even for long-term disciples who have been running the race faithfully for years, there can be questions on how to deal with surprising new challenges. And real-life factors may be in the mix, such as getting older, changes that come with menopause, having children, being married, losing a job, trying to find a job, being in school, having adult children, being lonely, and conflict in relationships.

"Do not fear...," "Do not be anxious...," "Do not be discouraged...," "Do not be afraid...," "Do not worry...." The Scriptures are full of words such as these. In fact, there are somewhere between 120 to 150 different instances of these kinds of phrases, depending on how you count them. So how should we respond to feelings of fear, tension, worry, and discouragement? People come to see me as a therapist for any number of reasons. Two of the most common are getting help with anxiety or having symptoms of depression. People share about troubling emotions of anger, anxiety, irritation, fear, frustration, and sadness. In my own learning on how to help people specifically with fear and anxiety, I have been drawn back again and again to the Scriptures, wanting to understand how God himself would have us work through these kinds of feelings.

People often tell me how they respond to these feelings. "I just pray until it goes away." "I just ignore it." "I get rid of them." "I cast them out." "I talk myself down." One of the most popular verses quoted is "Take captive every thought" (2 Corinthians 10:5).

Let's look at that scripture. An important thing to note is that this verse in 2 Corinthians is not about our fearful hearts, or about the anxiety sentence that just went through your head. If one were to read the whole letter, it becomes clear that the Apostle Paul is referring to the words of false teachers. Paul here is pointing out how "every thought" of false prophets needs to be held up against, taken captive by, the Scriptures. The Corinthians, and by extension we, are called to examine teachings that are contrary to the gospel by carefully comparing them to the truths in God's word. So this passage is about dealing with false teaching. It is not about dealing with the fearful, anxious thoughts in your head. Why is that important?

Many faithful, Bible-loving Christians have been trying to take their thoughts captive by clamping down on them, shutting them up with Scripture, and feeling guilty or bad about being faithless. Using those kinds of images may have worked for some reading here, but for many, you unfortunately find that those thoughts you believe you took captive continue plaguing you again and again, even though you've confessed, quoted Scripture, and told yourself those thoughts are wrong. And these strategies have not gotten rid of those worries and fears for you. You may have been told you are faithless, that your fear is a sin, and that your anxiety is the opposite of faith; that since Jesus rebuked people for their lack of faith, you are in sin when you are anxious. And yet...the thoughts come back. The feelings keep popping back in. And you keep trying the same way of dealing with them.

It may be important to consider that taking your thoughts captive is not what God intends for how to deal with your thoughts and feelings. It's not what Paul is teaching in 2 Corinthians 10.

You may have been telling yourself, or others may have told you, some of the following things:

- You need to be positive.

- You need to move on.

- You need to stop dwelling on the negative.

- You just need to be confident.

- It doesn't do you any good to stay stuck on that.

- You need to get past that.

- You need to take it captive.

- Don't let Satan win.

- You need to be calm (this is one of the *worst*).

I would contend, first, that God does not respond to our feelings in these kinds of dismissive ways ("Get rid of it" or "Get it under control"). I also contend another important point: These feelings have something important to say, and when someone ignores them or shoves them in some dark hole, it doesn't work. And it doesn't give these important feelings a chance to have a voice and talk.

Consider this: Your distressing feelings of fear and anxiety may have something important to say, and instead of being shut up, they may just need to talk to someone who will listen. God would.

Think of it this way: If a friend came to you and expressed his fears and worries, would you try to get rid of him? If she began to share with you something she was worried about, would you just ignore her? When your friend started talking, would you just spontaneously start praying, not looking at them, even walking away from them, and continuing to pray until they left the room? Of course not.

If you're a parent, a grandparent, an auntie or uncle, a children's ministry worker, when your little ones come running in, all distressed, do you tell them to leave? "You need to leave!" Or do you say, "Come here" and have them sit on your lap? Most people I ask say the latter. My clients tell me they get down on that young child's level, they take their hand, they speak in a soothing voice, they listen.

We might have many ways we respond to someone's fears and anxieties and sadness, but one thing most of us wouldn't do is ignore them, walk away from them, tell them to leave, or tell them that they are not wanted and should stop. We listen. It is true that we might also engage in some problematic responses like trying to fix too soon. Every married couple knows how well that goes. When someone—a friend, a sibling, a coworker, or a spiritual sister/brother—shares, we might be dismissive of the fear in some way after listening. We might say, "Trust God" before drawing out their concern. But even in our worst moments, we don't turn our back. We don't refuse to listen. Well, at least rarely.

Now think of your feelings as a being, a person. How do you treat your feelings when they walk in wanting to talk with you? Most of you reading here probably have more compassion for your friends or children who come to share these things with you than you do for your own feelings and thoughts. Most of you are quicker to shut down your own fear than you are to shut down a friend who expresses that very same feeling. What would it be like to have compassion with your own feelings? This is usually an important first step in figuring out what to do with distressing feelings. Have compassion. On yourself. God does.

Let's consider how God is. The Scriptures teach us God is "the Father of compassion and the God of all comfort" (2 Corinthians 1:3). "In all their distress, he too was distressed" (Isaiah 63:9). "He took note of their distress when he heard their cry" (Psalm 106:44). God has compassion on us. He cares and he listens. Wait... slow down, and go back and read those scriptures again. Read them slowly. Ponder them. Read them and say them out loud slowly. Sit with them for a moment. No, truly, stop reading here and go back and look at each of them and meditate on each one.

Do you see God's compassion? And how are you doing having that same compassion on yourself? How are you doing responding to your own troubling emotions? Are you kind like God? When a troubling emotion, such as fear, anger, hurt, sadness, anxiety, or worry walks into your room, do you respond to it like God would? Take more time to look at God's kindness, patience, and compassion. Do a thorough study of the Scriptures. And then consider what might happen if you were to respond to those emotions the same way God does when they walk in.

Acceptance

An idea I use to describe this process of learning a new way to respond to our thoughts, feelings, and those pesky body responses is the concept of *acceptance*. Acceptance is the idea of a willingness and openness to your whole experience, embracing rather than rejecting these parts of yourself. God does give each of us the opportunity to choose the direction we want to move with our thoughts and feelings, but he first and foremost has empathy and compassion about what we think and feel. Acceptance is the opportunity to step into God's heart about you and who you are on the inside.

Most of the time when we have a thought or feeling that we don't feel good about (or especially when someone else has a thought or feeling we don't feel good about), we want to fix it. With negative emotions, we want to do whatever it takes to feel okay, which of course often leads us to feeling even less okay. It is amazing how dismissing a thought or a feeling just makes most of us feel worse or makes the thought or feeling stronger. So ask yourself, when you try to get rid of that worry or negative thought or emotion, is it working? When you try to avoid uncomfortable emotions, does it work?

The reality is that painful emotions and difficult thoughts are universal, and for many of us, the struggle to avoid or get rid of them leads to suffering. There is a misconception that we have some kind of control switch for our internal experiences. "Don't think of a yellow jeep." Stop thinking of the yellow jeep! For many of us, the more we struggle with a problematic thought, the more stuck we become. Perhaps there is a better way.

Acceptance, being able to say to yourself, "That is understandable" when you have that thought and feeling, and then having compassion on yourself, a kind of *self-compassion,* may be a new road to take. Consider that as we look at a few more things.

Mindfulness

Let's continue this chapter with two practical, spiritual exercises. A mindful practice is the first. And a scriptural turning toward our beliefs and values is another.

Think of a situation recently that was troublesome to you. Something within the last week or so. Don't choose something traumatic or overwhelmingly huge. Think of something that moderately bothered you and it still clings a bit. You may want to take time to write it down in a journal, or even on your computer, tablet, or phone. After you identify the situation, recognize what thoughts go through your head about that situation.

Note the specific sentences that you say internally. Write them down. Really. Slow down and follow my direction here. Write the sentences down that go through your head. Not paragraphs. Just a couple individual sentences you associate with that moderately bothersome situation. Now ask yourself, how do you feel about it? What emotion words match. I have added a section at the end here of different emotion words if you need help identifying your feelings. Choose a few.

Now read the sentences again and let yourself notice the feelings that come up. Write the words down and the feeling words that match. Now close your eyes and take a look inside. Pay attention to the way your body is responding. As you let yourself feel and think about the situation, as you read the words you wrote down, what do you notice in your body? In your chest, in your stomach, on your shoulders, on your forehead, in your neck, do you notice anything?

Now as you notice these responses, I want to caution you, don't try to fix it or disciple yourself. You may feel the desire to judge yourself and whether you should think and feel that way. But see if you can just notice the sensations in your body as you allow yourself to give some attention to the thoughts and feelings. You do not have to decide right now if what you feel or think is good or bad, right or wrong. You are just being an observer.

Now breathe. Deeply, in your nose and out your mouth. Long and slow. Let the breath go deep into your lungs. Take a few deep breaths. Now let yourself observe and notice your thoughts, your feelings, and the sensations in your body. And continue to breathe as you do it. They don't have to go away. You don't have to do anything about them. Just notice them. And breathe.

This is a small step of mindfulness, nonjudgmental noticing. It would take a book-length reading to walk through where to go from here (this chapter is part of a larger book I am writing right now), but for now, we are just going to be mindful of the thoughts, the feelings, and the bodily sensations. And just accept them as they are with a free breath.

"I Am with You"

Above, we practiced mindfulness. Nonjudgmental noticing. Acceptance of your feelings, thoughts, and sensations. In this section, we are going to take one emotion and walk into the Scriptures with it. Fear.

Say the phrase "Do not fear." Say it out loud as you are reading this. Now say it again, and this time let it be the beginning of a sentence from God or from a scripture you've heard.

"Do not fear…"

"Do not fear, because…"

Say that sentence out loud. When you think of God saying that to you, "Do not fear, because…," how does that sentence finish in your mind? In the Scriptures, how does God finish that sentence: "Do not fear, because…"? Pause and think about that before you read on. How does the sentence from God continue: "Do not fear, because…"?

Do you have an answer in your head? Don't read on until you do.

Many people I speak to who have some knowledge of the Scriptures answer this in a similar way: "Do not fear, because I AM WITH YOU" (Isaiah 41:10). Or something close to that. There are several different ways that God finishes that sentence and others like it. But let's sit with this first one for just a minute.

Do not fear, because I am with you.

I am with you.

Look carefully at those words. Don't read on. Sit and look at those italicized words and let them just rest inside you. Go do it right now. Hear God say them. As you read them hear his voice say them. Read them and just look at them and sit.

Now take a full minute and put your eyes on those words again, and as you look at them, just let yourself breathe. Just breathe deeply, a low belly breath, and hear God say these words to you multiple times. When other thoughts come in, let them float through. Let your mind stay focused on those words for a full minute.

*****

I hope you paused and slowed down and followed the above direction. If you didn't, please stop reading and go do it. Go meditate on God's words.

As I typed this section, trying to figure out how to convey to my readers the importance of this one phrase, I sat and just looked at the words myself, and I could feel many things: a bit overwhelmed, relief, longing, gratitude, sadness. I felt a smile come on. I felt tears as well. I had to breathe more. God says to me, "I am with you." Like you, there are any number of things that I fear, that make me sad, that feel hard, painful, difficult, and sometimes overwhelming. And the God of the universe says to me, "I am with you."

To close out our time together, let me encourage you with something. The next time you have a troubled thought or feeling, slow down and notice how it shows up. Think about saying to that thought or feeling, to yourself, like you would to someone you love, "That's understandable. I understand why you're here."

There really are some legitimate reasons you are having that feeling, reasons that thought is going through your head. Though you may wish you could just get rid of that anxiety, there are things in your upbringing, in your background, or that are happening in your life now, that make it truly understandable that anxiety has walked in and is wanting to talk to you right now. So consider having a new relationship with that thought or feeling. Maybe even say hi to it. Give it a hug. No, really. It has walked in. Say hi and give it a hug.

Rather than trying to shove it down or get rid of it, try something different. It has come to visit you so many times through the years. And here it is today, wanting to talk. Perhaps you can show it the kind of compassion God would. And then, as you give it that hug, you can turn your mind toward your belief in the God you love, the Father of compassion and the God of all comfort. And as you sit with kindness next to that anxiety that has walked in, hear him say to you, "Fear not, for I am with you." And let yourself breathe.

Resources

David Takle, MDiv, *Whispers of my Abba: From His Heart to Mine* (High Point, NC: Kingdom Formation, 1996).

CHAPTER SEVEN

Presencing and Discernment

Diana Steer, OT

Diana Steer is a practitioner of spiritual direction, having received formal training at Hesichya School of Spiritual Direction, a long-established training program in contemplative, evocative, and interfaith methods of spiritual direction. Spiritual direction is the art of deep listening in service to others in their personal journey of the long walk of faith into a deeper and vibrant relationship with God. It also is a nonjudgmental approach to hope and healing. The practice of presencing provides greater awareness to the presence of the Holy Spirit as it works within us. For disciples who feel a need to revive their relationship with God, the practices of spiritual direction and presencing are offered at the sabbath spiritual retreats in Alaska at Gateway to the Arctic. You may contact Diana should you be considering obtaining a spiritual director: DianaSteer.22@gmail.com.

Diana L-Steffen Steer, MA
Spiritual director — contemplative, evocative
Author, retreat leader — Gateway to the Arctic (G2A)
Organizational Leadership, Servant-Leadership (R. Greenleaf)
Occupational therapist, retired

Spiritual Direction, Deep Listening, Presencing, and Discernment

In this chapter you will learn how spiritual direction, deep listening, and presencing inform discernment. Through personal and biblical examples, you will develop an understanding and the use of these spiritual disciplines. You will also have access to the presencing process, which you can try in a small group of four or five individuals. We have found in our fellowship that this process, even in an online format, has built relationships and an openness with one another that would not have occurred otherwise.

My Story

I became a disciple in 1982 and could not get enough of God's word, fellowship, prayer time, and sharing God's word with others. As a nontraditional college student, I loved being in the campus ministry and mostly flourished spiritually for the next eight years. I married, adopted a child, and served on two mission teams.

Entry into my desert began when my sister died in a kayaking accident and there were numerous challenging church leadership changes, along with a variety of other influences. When my husband and I were no longer in positions of church responsibilities, I did not know who I was; I was hurt, lost, and withdrawn. I felt that if my talents and skills were not going to be used in the kingdom, then I would use them elsewhere.

I threw myself into university art classes, worked two jobs, and generally lost any interest in church functions and my relationship with God, though I continued to show up and was willing to get with various friends in the church. My husband and I were always described as good soldiers and considered low maintenance. I went along with this; we didn't ask for help.

Meanwhile I continued walking through my spiritual desert, though there were a few oases. A sister recommended I investigate a master's program where I decided to enroll in the Organizational Leadership program with a concentration in Servant-Leadership as developed by Robert Greenleaf. This is where I encountered the concepts I am presenting here. Ironically, the university I was working for and the university I attended were both Jesuit, so service to God underlay all that I learned. My relationship with God began to come alive, but it wasn't until Shane and Sara Engel, I, and others began working on the Alaska Sabbath Retreats that I recognized the way God was present in my life.

Offering presencing at these retreats and within our fellowship really drew me out of the desert; I found the unique ways I could contribute to God's kingdom. Additionally, I learned of and am now formally trained as a spiritual director, having started an online practice. I also obtained a spiritual director and a spiritual supervisor according to best practices of spiritual direction. In this journey, I also learned that as we mature and transition through life, our spiritual life also transitions in a way that no longer meets our spiritual needs. I found this to be quite unsettling until it was addressed as I trained as a spiritual director. The spiritual desert feels far in the distance, and my relationship with God is fresh, creative, and growing; I can say that I am having the time of my life making new friends in the kingdom and watching God move in the lives of others. I really believe God was with me in the desert, just as the angels attended Jesus (Mark 1:12–13).

Spiritual Direction

Spiritual direction is a spiritual discipline first practiced in the 1400s and documented by Theresa of Avila and John of the Cross. They each maintained a deep and prayerful spirituality and a lyrical friendship in which they expressed their love for God, times of God's seeming absence during spiritual deserts, and sharing their joys and sorrows in service to others. Spiritual direction is not about being directed, but rather about being encouraged to draw closer to God: how he shows up in your life, and a recognition of his presence and grace.

Some benefits of spiritual direction are the ability to identify and trust your own experiences of God, integrate spirituality in your daily life, discern, make difficult choices, and live the essence of your spiritual affiliation with integrity. A spiritual director, soul companion, or soul friend joins with you in the journey of your life for the purpose of revealing God's presence to you and helping you to draw nearer to him throughout that journey.[40]

Personal Experience

In spiritual direction, I have been able to explore several cherished "unexplainable mysteries of God" that I had experienced

---

40. See www.sdiworld.org for further information.

in childhood, in a caring and sensitive way. Working with the Enneagram, I have been able to work with my spiritual director around personal characteristics that undergird several of my behaviors, recurring sin, and decision-making processes. We have also shared about our beloved dogs and end-of-life issues. In talking with someone I do not have frequent contact with (once a month), I feel a sense of safety and freedom from judgment to talk about deep matters. I lead the discussion, and my spiritual director asks me questions that help evoke related emotions, patterns, and choices that I may not be aware of.

Biblically, I am reminded of the devotion that Jonathan had for David (1 Samuel 18:3–4), and Ruth for Naomi (Ruth 1:16–18).

Listening Deeply

Listening occurs on four different levels, according to Otto Scharmer:[41]

Level I: Downloading (common exchange of information)
Level II: Factual (scientific—only the facts, please)
Level III: Empathic (feeling from another's point of view)
Level IV: Generative listening (exchange of dialogue connecting to future possibilities)

Example: The Samaritan Woman (John 4:4–26)
You are a Jew, and I am a Samaritan. – Downloading
Sir, you have nothing to draw with. – Factual
You are right when you say you have no husband. – Empathic
A time is coming when you will worship the Father. – Generative: future possibilities

These distinctions are important, as deep listening is essential in the presencing and discerning process. Deep listening requires that we have the same mindset as Jesus, making ourselves nothing,

---

41. Otto Scharmer is a senior lecturer in the MIT Sloan School of Management and cofounder of the Presencing Institute. He chairs the MIT IDEAS program for cross-sector innovation and introduced the concept of "presencing"—learning from the emerging future—in his bestselling books *Theory U* and *Presence* (the latter coauthored with Peter Senge and others).

taking the nature of a servant, completely humble and valuing others above ourselves without selfish ambition or vain conceit (Philippians 2:1–11).

The reason this mindset is so important is because it allows us to be present to the individual we are listening to and while listening for the voice of God and watching for the openings God may be providing. These openings are clues to deeper truths and, when addressed through gentle open-ended questioning, can lead to a greater authenticity and closeness in one's relationship with God. Spiritual directors are trained to watch and listen for these openings, but it is possible for an unpracticed individual to recognize them. When this happens in the presencing process and when there is an observable shift in the individual's awareness, it is understood that there is a connection with the Spirit of God and a sense of an emerging future, just as Jesus promised the Samaritan woman.

During this time, it is important to refrain from downloading or factual forms of questioning, giving the person a chance to experience the emotions and feelings of their body in their new awareness. From this position and through generative dialogue, discernment generally comes easily and with a deep sense of confidence, freedom, and trust.

Discernment

Does your new awareness draw you farther from God or closer to God? Making a decision is not the goal of spiritual discernment, but rather, does the decision *root you deeper in Christlikeness or just satisfy a self-serving desire?* Regardless of the final action, God can help us work through it and teach us valuable lessons (Ephesians 3:20). In the presencing process, we can have a deep sense of a decision's rightness.

Personal Experience

I had been encouraged by my faculty to pursue a doctoral degree, and I was really tempted to do so. However, doing so, in my mind, would require relocating to a new congregation and a new community, and displacing or separating from my spiritual family for a time. I was excited by the thought of continuing my education and essentially living closer to my biological family. My pride was aroused by the attention I was receiving. Emotionally, I was all in for the future I envisioned for myself. Utilizing presencing gave me the opportunity to make a more definitive decision.

My coaches/compassionate listeners listened deeply and asked me open-ended nonjudgmental or leading questions as I presented my case clinic to them. At times, their questioning caused me to wince and my body to tense as they were getting closer to the heart of the matter. I began to recognize my selfishness and self-serving desires. I had to question the financial and relational pressure a decision like this would place on my church community, my family, and my own spirituality.

Once I owned my sinful desires, I started to let go of my perceived future. Then, one of my coaches asked me to explain why I felt pursuing a doctoral degree and moving had to be one decision, dependent on one another, when they were separate issues. For whatever reason, I had not considered this, and the rightness of this new awareness was like finally bringing my binoculars into focus. The feeling was so intense and sensible that I was able to let go of my imagined future without regret or a sense of loss. I felt a deep connection to the presence of God and to not pursue my education, or to pressure my family felt so thoroughly aligned with God's will that I had no doubt or reservations. I was aware that I was making a godly decision. It has been several years since I used the process of presencing to discern my future, and I have never doubted letting go of what I held so dear. More importantly, I have appreciated the awareness of my sinful selfishness and self-serving pride. My repentance is real and long lasting, thanks to God and the process of discernment (2 Corinthians 7:8–13).

Presencing Process

The process of presencing was developed by Scharmer[42] as the second movement of Theory U. It is used with permission and

---

42. https://www.presencing.org/aboutus/theory-u

adapted for spiritual purposes. According to Scharmer, presencing is understood as "connection to source"—a way of knowing, otherwise God. The steps are easy to follow with individuals who are willing to trust and to stay within the guidelines. Generative dialogue involves all participants creating and exploring new possibilities together.

Case Clinic Exercise (Approx. 70 min per session, 4 or 5 persons per team) © 2013 Presencing Institute – www.Presencing.org

Note: *Entering the exercise, you are standing on sacred and confidential ground. Nothing shared is open for discussion outside the session unless the case giver initiates it.*

Roles:

1. **Case Giver:** Share your personal aspiration and challenge that is current, concrete, and important, of which you happen to be a key player. It can be presented in fifteen minutes and could make a big difference in your future. Include your personal learning threshold (what you need to let go of and learn).

2. **Coaches/Compassionate Listeners:** Listen deeply— do not try to "fix" the problem, but rather listen deeply to the case giver while also attending to the images, metaphors, feelings, and gestures that the story evokes in you. Also consider nonverbal communication such as emotional breaks in voice, wistfulness in eyes, etc.

3. **Generative Scriber:** Someone who will document input and ideas beneficial to the Case Giver.

4. **Timekeeper:** One of the coaches manages the time and maintains compliance with the process.

Procedure:

1. Select case giver and timekeeper (2 min); everyone but the case giver is a coach/compassionate listener.

2. Case giver intention statement (15 min): *Take a moment*

to reflect on your sense of calling. Then clarify these questions (timekeeper may prompt):

a. Current situation: What key challenge or question are you up against?

    Intention: What future are you trying to create?

b. Learning edge: What do you need to let go of, and what do you need to learn?

c. Help: Where do you need input or help?

    Coaches listen deeply and may ask clarifying questions (avoid giving advice, interpreting, or contributing your story).

3. Stillness (3 min): Do not compromise the 3 minutes.

    a. All listen to your heart: Connect with your heart to what you are hearing—listen to what resonates.

    b, What images, metaphors, feelings, drawings, or gestures come up for you that capture the essence of what you heard?

4. Mirroring images (20 min): Creative process

    a. Each coach shares images, metaphors, feelings, drawings, or gestures that captured the essence of the case situation. Be succinct.

    b. Case giver listens for images, feelings, insights, etc.

5. Generative dialogue (20 min): (All participants contribute)

    a. Continue the conversation, starting with the case giver having listened to the mirroring by others; the case giver reflects and shares the meanings of what these images, stories, and collective gestures evoke: *Viewing myself from the distance, what touched me, what resonated with me, what questions and reflections come up for me now?*

    b. All reflect on case giver's remarks and move into generative dialogue, exploring new perspectives and views on what was revealed in relationship to the case giver's story.

    c. Stay in service to the case giver, avoiding advice, comparison of personal stories, etc.

6. Closing remarks (8 min):
   a. Coaches thank case giver.
   b. Case giver shares: *How do they see their way forward, and their situation now?*
   c. Thank you: Express ppreciation to each other
7. Individual journaling to capture the learning points (2–5 minutes)

Subtleties and Personal Experience

The first time I served as a teacher's assistant for a graduate program, my presencing group experienced a huge disruption caused by one of the participants. Their behavior disrupted the entire cohort of twenty students. I was devastated and felt like a failure. However, the instructor was very supportive of my efforts and explained that this student was not at all prepared to be in the course despite weeks of preparation. Thankfully, I did not give up and learned more from this experience than I ever could otherwise. The student did eventually come back but joined another group, never giving their case clinic.

That time formed in me a greater effort to rely on prayer, my senses, and intuition, and to honor the decision someone else makes. Presencing is integrated into my conversations, especially when someone is sharing something intimate to them. For example, a family member could not decide whether she wanted to move into an assisted living facility or remain in her home. Conversationally, I used the presencing process and listened deeply, asking clarifying open-ended questions. During the conversation, she was able to make a confident and freeing decision to move into assisted living and has not changed her mind since we had this conversation. In teaching, serving various-sized groups, participating in retreats, and in an online format, I have been able to develop nuances unique to my style of interaction with others; it is not a restrictive process. The following is an example of a participant's experience with the presencing process.

A Case Clinic – Dr. Timothy Sumerlin as the case giver

In September 2021 at the Sabbath Spiritual Retreat at Gateway to the Arctic, north of Anchorage, Alaska, I (Tim) was privileged to participate as a case giver in a presencing exercise led by Diana Steer. It was a life-giving exercise for me, and almost a year later, it still has a positive impact on my soul.

Several therapists and attendees gathered around a fireplace and asked for a volunteer—I eagerly raised my hand, as I had something on my heart. I will not disclose the specific nature of my issue, only that it was family related. As I shared my problem and difficulty in my heart and thinking, it became apparent that this was indeed a problem for me and one that I had been stuck in for a while. Diana Steer began to lead the group through the above-mentioned exercise.

Everyone in the room had a comment about what God had shared with them concerning my issue. I was astounded at the accuracy of detail as they shared their thoughts with me. Many tears were shared, emotion was present, and important nuances of my issue were communicated. I walked away with some very solid considerations and stirring responses with many of the comments.

After reflecting on this in the ensuing days on prayer walks and other times of contemplation, I gained valuable encouragement, peace, and insight into my issue. I am forever grateful for this experience and hope it is a blessing to you as well!

Conclusion

The presencing process and case clinic exercise is incredibly powerful. It has the capacity to help participants shift a paradigm, change perspectives, make difficult life decisions, and make friends of strangers. It is an adaptable and nuanced process capable of reaching a wide range of audiences and taps into our deepest character, drawing us into God's love and intimacy. It is not a process that is right for all individuals due to its imaginative, sensory, and insightful approach. Additionally, participants may not be ready to let go of a seemingly obvious obstacle or the past and may be reluctant to embrace the emerging future that the presencing process can reveal. It is not for us to push them or try to make a point; it is their journey. Humility and trust is key to its success. It is a process focused on the emerging future, which can be threatening to those who struggle with change.

Silence is essential to the process as well and can be used to refocus the group, but it is especially important following the case clinic exercise. This is the place where we can hear God's voice and is also a place of reflection and healing. Silence has been a welcome addition to many of my conversations because of its calming and organizing properties. I hope you will try facilitating the case clinic exercise with several of your friends so that you can learn and utilize the process. Remember that when you engage in the case clinic exercise, you are standing on sacred ground and all aspects are *confidential and closed to any discussion beyond the exercise* unless the case giver initiates the conversation. This is without exception. You are welcome to contact me if you have questions or would like to talk with me further about spiritual direction or the presencing process.

Resources

David G. Benner, *Sacred Companions: The Gift of Spiritual Friendship and Direction* (Downers Grove, IL: InterVarsity, 2002).

Theresa Blythe, *Spiritual Direction 101: the basics of spiritual guidance* (Berkeley, CA: Apocryphile, 2018).

John Henry Horsman, *Servant-Leaders in Training* (Switzerland: Palgrave MacMillan, 2018).

William Johnston (Ed.), *The Cloud of Unknowing* (New York, NY: Doubleday, 1973).

Gerald G. May, *The Dark Night of the Soul* (New York, NY: HarperCollins, 2004).

Henri Nouwen, *Discernment: Reading the Signs of Daily Life* (San Francisco, CA: HarperOne, 2013).

Henri Nouwen, *Spiritual Direction: Wisdom for the Long Walk of Faith* (San Francisco, CA: HarperOne, 2006).

R. J. Sardello, *Silence: the Mystery of Wholeness* (Berkeley, CA: Goldenstone, 2008).

C. O. Scharmer and K. Kaufer, *Leading from the Emerging Future: From Ego-System To Eco-System Economics* (San Francisco, CA: Berrett-Kohler, 2013).

Otto Scharmer, *The Essentials of Theory U: Core Principles and Applications* (San Francisco, CA: Berrett-Kohler, 2018).

Spiritual Directors International. Guidelines for ethical conduct: SDI. www.sdicompanions.org

David Takle, *Forming: a Work of Grace* (High Point, NC: Kingdom Formation, 2013).

Dallas Willard, *The Spirit of the Disciplines: Understanding How God Changes Lives* (United Kingdom: HarperCollins, 1988).

www.presencing.org

CHAPTER EIGHT

Lectio Divina:
The Word Becomes Life

Dr. Tracy Jones, EdD and LaShell Pope, LMFT

Dr. Tracy Jones is a member of the Boston Church of Christ and has been a disciple since 1996. She is married and has four children. She received a master's in counseling psychology from Lesley University and a doctoral degree in the field of Christian counseling from Liberty University. Her research has been in using Christian meditation to treat anxiety, depression, and shame. She has been a clinician since 1997 and is a member of the executive management team at CrossPoint Clinical Services, a faith-based counseling and wellness nonprofit. Tracy enjoys hiking, cheering on her kids in their various endeavors, traveling, reading, and drinking tea. She has a passion for helping people see God's love and listen to his Spirit by learning to be quiet in his presence. Her favorite scripture is Exodus 14:14: "The Lord will fight for you, you need only to be still."

Tracy Jones, EdD, LPC, LMHC, CMIP www.crosspointclinical.org

Lectio divina is a devout practice of the ancient desert mothers and fathers that can be used by Christians today to inspire a profound intimacy with God and a greater understanding of the work of the Holy Spirit through the word of God. It was first defined by Benedict of Nursia, Italy, the founder of the Benedictine monks. In his book, *The Rule,* written in 540, he describes lectio divina, Latin for "sacred or divine reading," as a means of meditation, prayer, and contemplation based on a holy reading of Scripture, the purpose of which is to help a believer gain a closer walk with God by taking a small passage of Scripture and allowing it to move in their heart. Earlier practitioners of this spiritual practice alternated randomly between reading, contemplation, meditation, and prayer, but during the Middle Ages, a monk named Guigo II who lived in France developed a metaphor to help guide times of lectio divina. He described it as a ladder with a specific starting point on earth and specific ending point in heaven. "We begin," he writes, "on earth, reading God's word. Then we climb the rungs of meditation and prayer, finally arriving in the clouds of heaven in contemplation."[43] These elements of lectio divina are designed to allow a person to develop a closer relationship with the divine by communing with God and understanding him more deeply through his word.

Guigo stated:

> Reading seeks, meditation finds, prayer asks, contemplation feels.... "Seek and you shall find: knock and the door will be opened for you" (Matthew 7:7). That means also, seek through reading, and you will find holy meditation in your thinking; and knock through praying, and the doors shall be opened to you to enter through heavenly contemplation to feel what you desire.[44]

Whether you choose to use them randomly or in a structured manner, let's explore the four basic steps of lectio divina.

Lectio – Reading

Lectio, the reading of Scripture, is not intended as a way to ingest substantial portions of the Word, but rather as a way to savor a small portion and to allow the Holy Spirit to guide you, the one engaged in this sacred reading, to a deeper understanding at a heart level. All Scripture is God-breathed and is suitable for lectio divina, but you may want to use the psalms as a starting point, as they tend to be devotional in content. This way of reading Scripture will not lend to increasing a cultural or contextual meaning, nor is it a biblical exegesis; it is a prayerful contemplation of the Word that facilitates a deep connection to God.

In preparation for this reading, it is recommended to choose

---

43. Tony Jones, *Divine Intervention* (Colorado: THINK, 2006), 51.

44. Tony Jones, *Divine Intervention*, 53.

a place that is quiet and free from distractions and a posture that is conducive to being alert to the presence of God. Then take a moment of silence to center the mind on the reading and to welcome the guidance of the Holy Spirit by purposely quieting and opening the mind. The mind will inevitably wander throughout your lectio divina time, and when it does, gently bring it back to the phase you are in without judgment or condemnation. 1 Corinthians 2:9–10 teaches:

> *"What no eye has seen,*
> *what no ear has heard,*
> *and what no human mind has conceived"—*
> *the things God has prepared for those who love him—*
> *these are the things God has revealed to us by his Spirit.*
> *The Spirit searches all things, even the deep things of God.*

This way of prayerful reading invites the Holy Spirit to direct the reader to a word or scriptural phrase to focus on more intently. In the phase of lectio, you are encouraged to read the passage of Scripture slowly and repeatedly, aloud and silently. You can read the same translation or multiple, but you are to listen for the prompting of the Holy Spirit, to notice which word or phrase you are drawn to bring your attention to more fully. The number of times you repeat this reading of the scripture, slowly and intentionally, will vary, but listen for the persuading to be pulled to a specific portion. *Lectio is a way to seek the presence of God in the word of God.*

Meditatio – Meditation

Meditatio is the meditation on the word or scriptural phrase that you have been led to focus on more intently. This phase allows you to focus on the small portion to mine the application it has for your life and to understand why you have been pulled to it today. Meditation helps you listen to the prompting of the Holy Spirit as it applies the Word to your heart and mind. It increases your understanding, as Psalm 119:97–99 says:

> *Oh, how I love your law!*
> *I meditate on it all day long.*

> *Your commands are always with me*
> *and make me wiser than my enemies.*
> *I have more insight than all my teachers,*
> *for I meditate on your statutes.*

This phase in lectio divina allows you to chew on the Word; to taste and slowly, deliberately savor it; and thereby notice its meaning for you. Meditation is not an empty or passive state, but an active one that promotes increased attention to and awareness of the Word. Although it is not an intellectual study of the scripture or word, it is a pondering and sitting with the passage and its personal meaning for you. It is a way to move a scripture from the brain to the heart where it can stimulate your thoughts and actions.

Oratio – Prayer

Oratio is the bringing of the Scripture word or phrase to God in prayer. Prayer is communication with God, a speaking, and a listening. Psalm 66:19 says, "God has surely listened and has heard my prayer." This is the phase in which one asks for help and where one listens for the reply. Prayer may lead to praise, petition, thanksgiving, or asking questions. It is meant to be a time to converse with God about what the reading and meditation has brought to your heart and mind, about how it has affected you, about who he is, and about who he wants you to be. You may notice your prayer shift as you continue, and it is important to progress slowly through this phase. You will benefit from leaving room for God's part of the conversation you are having with him. You will practice both being open and vulnerable and actively being attentive to listen.

Contemplatio – Contemplation

The listening part of your prayer may lead naturally into contemplatio, the contemplation or deep seeking element of lectio divina. We begin a practice of lectio divina hungry and thirsty for God, and in contemplation he comforts this, as it says in Psalm 107:8–9:

Let them give thanks to the LORD for his unfailing love
and his wonderful deeds for mankind,
for he satisfies the thirsty
and fills the hungry with good things.

This contemplation is a time of resting in God's presence, in his love and goodness. It is the point at which the Holy Spirit prays for us, in us, and through us as we sit in silent, restful prayer. 2 Corinthians 3:17–18 says, "Now the Lord is the Spirit, and where the Spirit of the Lord is, there is freedom. And we all, who with unveiled faces contemplate the Lord's glory, are being transformed into his image with ever-increasing glory, which comes from the Lord, who is the Spirit." No matter what word or scriptural phrase became your focus for the day, this time of contemplation is a time of resting in God's care and in his infinite love for you.

Lectio divina can be done as an individual experience or in a group, you can use an app or a book as a guide, it can be done unstructured or structured, but it is a practice. Like all spiritual practices, it becomes more effective the more you practice it. As a reminder, with any contemplative or meditative exercise, it is natural to experience a wandering of the mind. Give yourself permission to redirect your thoughts back repeatedly and gently to your sacred reading and reenter the phase you are in at the time. You may find this happens less the longer you have been doing it. If you have never tried lectio divina before, enter into it with curiosity and suspend judgment toward yourself. Allow yourself to try something new in this ancient approach to seeking deeper meaning through God's divine word.

Let us now look at an example of how lectio divina can be used in a church setting.

Group Lectio Divina
LaShell R. Pope LMFT

LaShell Pope is a native of Dayton, Ohio and a graduate of Wright State University with a bachelor's degree in business communication and a master's in marriage and family therapy from Amridge University. Over the last twenty-two years, God has provided her with opportunities to serve as a women's ministry leader and hospice chaplain in various churches and hospices throughout metro Atlanta and Savannah, GA, and Southern California. As a licensed marriage and family therapist, LaShell also works in private practice currently offering tele-mental health and bereavement counseling in Marietta, Georgia. LaShell and her husband, Michael, have two daughters, Evan and Erin.

> *May these words of my mouth and this meditation of my heart*
>   *be pleasing in your sight,*
> *LORD, my Rock and my Redeemer.* (Psalm 19:14)

Keep this Book of the Law always on your lips; meditate on it day and night, so that you may be careful to do everything written in it. Then you will be prosperous and successful. (Joshua 1:8)

> *I meditate on your precepts*
>   *and consider your ways.* (Psalm 119:15)

Ten years ago, the ministry staff that my husband and I were a part of began to discuss the importance of practicing spiritual formation and disciplines in our own lives as well as helping our congregation to mature in these areas. Our journey began by enrolling in biblical education courses and taking Christian counseling classes that focused on the history and practice of spiritual formation and disciplines. Spiritual formation is defined as the process of transformational growth by becoming more like Jesus. Spiritual disciplines are the practices of those transformational processes that aid our growth and continue to deepen our relationship with God. Through our studies, the spiritual discipline of lectio divina was discovered.

Lectio divina is an ancient Christian tradition that has been practiced by monks for many years. In the last several years, lectio divina has gained popularity among Christians who have found that it has helped them connect with and experience God's word on a much deeper level. While the main steps of lectio divina remain the same, most groups have additional steps with some sharing with group members. Here is a variation of group lectio divina:

- Silencio (Prepare): the group has an opportunity to center themselves through silence and stillness (Psalm 46:10).

- Lectio (Read): the first reading; the group writes a word or phrase that stands out to them and each shares with the group. No additional commentary.

- Meditatio (Reflect): the second reading; the group reflects and writes how the word or phrase might relate to them specifically or where they might find themselves in the scripture and each shares with the group.

- Oratio (Respond): the third reading; the group responds to how they are feeling about what has been revealed to them in silent prayer to God

- Contemplatio (Rest): the fourth reading; the group rests in silence about the previous steps.

- Incarnatio (Live it out): after the final reading, the group reflects and writes how they can apply or live out what has been revealed, then each shares with the group.

The first time I experienced a form of lectio divina in a group setting was during a leaders' retreat a few years ago. After we were divided into small groups, we were given a very brief scripture to read aloud several times. We then shared what words or phrases stood out to each of us individually, as well as determining if there were any common themes within our group. Finally, we all prayed together and felt a deep spiritual bond with one another afterward. Wow! I didn't see that coming; I don't think any of us did. I was new to the region and didn't know many of these women personally, but I was pleasantly surprised by the connection with one another during that time.

I immediately took the practice back to my ministry and did it with the women there. We carried out the same steps, and since I did have relationships with these women, the experience of bonding through meditating on God's word was even more powerful. This later led to my husband and me seeing the fruits of spiritual disciplines done in groups (silence, solitude, meditation, sabbath rest) and how the impact of these practices was transforming lives.

However, lectio divina has also had its critics. Some, like David Helm, caution that the practice "advocates a method that is spiritual as opposed to systematically studious. It substitutes intuition for investigation. It prefers mood and emotion to methodical and reasoned inquiry. It equates your spirit to the Holy Spirit." I must point out that Helm is referring to ministers properly preparing for preaching sermons. But I do agree that we should always remind everyone that any type of spiritual discipline, including group lectio divina, is only a tool to assist us with becoming more like Jesus and does not supersede God's word. In my personal experience, I have found this method didn't lead me to prefer mood and emotion over Bible study. On the contrary, I have gained a lot of insight through this practice, and it has led me to a much more in-depth Bible study. Reading, meditation, prayer, and contemplation of a scripture have prompted me to really listen to God's voice and not my own and to discern what God is asking or saying to me through his word, and will I respond in obedience.

When I study God's word, I try to ensure that I understand who the author was speaking to at the time, what was the author's intended message, and how can I apply that message to my life today. Having a clear and knowledgeable understanding of Scripture has enabled me to rest on God's assurances, not my own. An advocate of lectio divina wrote an article in response to critics. He points out that spiritual meditation of Scripture does not replace the importance of biblical study. Kyle Norman states, "It does not run contrary to the discipline of study. In fact, the discipline of biblical meditation is only enhanced by methodical study. The more we study a text, the more fruitful our meditations can be." I agree, and additionally, when this practice is done in a group setting, everyone can experience being significantly enlightened on a scripture by the insight of others as everyone shares their experience together. Having experienced and witnessed this, I can say it was immensely powerful!

I have since facilitated group lectio divina with several different churches, at retreats, in person, and over Zoom. Most of the people that have shared in this practice have walked away wanting to learn more about it and practice it on their own as well as experience it with other people. Here are some of the statements sisters have shared with me:

"The benefit of doing it in a group setting versus alone helped me to think deeper about what God was really saying to me after hearing what other sisters shared."

"I was intrigued by the practice of lectio divina. I believe it is better in a small group where one can share and reflect on what was said by the group. It was different from small group discussions because it focuses one on being still and listening for the prompting of the Holy Spirit."

"It was a peaceful and reflective time, and I love it."

"In a group, you get to hear how God speaks to each one of us while hearing the same scriptures. We get to grow deeper in our relationship with one another."

"The silence and being still was hard for me because my thoughts went all over the place. But I did like hearing what others gleaned."

Below are some key takeaways that I have learned that can help your group lectio divina experience to be successful:

- It is especially important to educate and give some background on lectio divina.

- Teach and/or remind your group that it is NOT a Bible study or discussion. The focus is not on cognitive learning, sharing ideas and opinions about the scripture.

- Understand the importance of creating a "safe place" so no one in the group feels judged, reassures, or gives advice, but everyone listens and silently prays for one another.

- The facilitator should present a calm and peaceful presence during the Scripture readings. This helps the group to feel more comfortable.

- Those who are new to the practice may struggle with sitting in silence or may wonder if they have done something incorrectly if a particular word or phrase doesn't stand out to them. Reassure them that this is a process, and nothing has been done wrong.

There are times the insight is deeper when practicing alone, while at other times your insight is deepened through hearing what others share. Either way lectio divina is done, the result is having the opportunity to grow closer to God, continue to be formed into Christ's image, and have deeper connections with those who share in the practice with you.

Resources

L. Boyer, "Guide to Lectio Divina," 2020, retrieved from Spirituality for Questioning Minds.

L. K. Fanucci, "The Practice of Group Lectio Divina," 2016, retrieved from communitiesofcalling.org.

D. Helm, *Expositional Preaching: How We Speak God's Word Today* (Wheaton, IL: Crossway, 2014).

K. Norman, "The Danger of Lectio Divina: My Response," 2017, https://revkylenorman.ca/2017/05/23/the-danger-of-lectio-divina-my-response/

CHAPTER NINE

The Journey:
Our Lifelong Spiritual Development

Robert Carrillo, MDiv

Robert Carrillo was born in Juarez Mexico and grew up in California. He was educated at the University of San Diego and San Diego State University, receiving a bachelor's degree in history. Later Robert studied at Pepperdine University where he received a master's in divinity. Robert and Michele have been married thirty-two years and have three adult children, Elena, Alexis, and Andrew. Robert and Michele entered the ministry as missionaries planting churches in Mexico City and Miami. He and Michele also led churches and ministries in Puerto Rico, Jamaica, and New York. After returning to San Diego, he and Michele led the San Diego church of Christ for seven years. Robert Carrillo served as CEO of HOPE worldwide for four years and now is finishing a doctorate in spiritual formation at Fuller Seminary. He is an evangelist and teacher with the Los Angeles church of Christ serving as part of the leadership team, as well as serving on the ICOC Teachers committee. *¡Buen camino!*

> You do not have a Soul,
> You are a Soul.
> You have a Body. —C.S. Lewis

> We are not human beings having a spiritual experience.
> We are spiritual beings having a human experience.
>   —Pierre Teilhard de Chardin

Many of us have more clearly developed plans for finances, further education, home improvements, and physical fitness than we do for our spiritual lives.   —Ruth Haley Barton

Spiritual Development

As we journey through life, we all pass through recognizable stages in psychological, emotional, and social development. Every stage, whether it is adolescence, middle age, or even the golden years, comes with its expectations and common manifestations of behavior, accomplishments, and struggles. We have common expectancies that everyone should "grow up" at some point in life and "act mature." Someone who is still emotionally immature at midlife worries those around them. We know that an immature adult can do great harm to others as well as to themselves. At the same time, we appreciate and admire a young person who is mature for their age, as someone who is mature beyond their years can be a great blessing to their family and friends. Generally, these things are known and recognized in life's journey. What we often fail to see or understand is the stages of spiritual development that are equally formational and of even greater importance in life's journey. There are clear and recognizable stages that every human being undergoes in their spiritual development.

Everyone has a spirit, a soul, that is being influenced and formed in some way. As disciples of Jesus, it is fundamental for our spiritual development to be healthy and to advance in Christ. Jesus promised life to the full, and he offered the light burden and easy yoke, promising rest for our souls and victory over sin, weakness, and fear. He is the way, the truth, and the life.[45] We are instant recipients of his mercy, grace, and forgiveness, but learning to live as the forgiven, loved, and empowered spirit is a lifelong process. Living the life of Jesus' promises is a slow, miraculous process. This is the wonderful life journey we are all on, whether we know it or not. The disciple's journey is an intentional journey of discovery and formation in Christ as we are transformed continually into his likeness and blessed to participate in his divine nature!

And we all, who with unveiled faces contemplate the Lord's glory, are being transformed into his image with ever-increasing glory, which comes from the Lord, who is the Spirit. (2 Corinthians 3:18)

---

45. In John 14:6, Jesus answered, "I am the way and the truth and the life. No one comes to the Father except through me."

Some History and Background

Although the focus on our spiritual development and formation is experiencing a wave of acceptance similar to a trend, it is certainly not a trend. Our spiritual journey has been the subject of deep study and contemplation since early Christianity. The New Testament letters are filled with direction for our spiritual journey. The early church fathers and mothers of the first centuries provided deep insights that gave direction to Christians in their times. In his classic writings, *Confessions,* the great African theologian, Augustine of Hippo, presents his autobiography and shares deep insights into the spiritual journey we all experience. Centuries later, Bernard of Clairvaux (1090–1153) presented an early model of the way we grow through the stages of love.[46]

Ignatius of Loyola was a pioneer of spirituality who discovered and formulated many spiritual disciplines that set standards that are a roadmap for many Christians even today. The Ignatian spirituality of prayer, contemplation, spiritual direction, discernment, and the daily Examen of Consciousness are studied and practiced by both Catholics and Protestants around the world. Teresa of Avila, the first woman doctorate of the church in the sixteenth century and a formidable leader of spirituality, set an amazing example of mature spirituality and inspires women around the world to this day. Her writings hold powerful and important truths about the way we grow spiritually. She influenced other great spiritual leaders, such as John of the Cross, who became a great spiritual teacher who influenced thousands over the centuries. They laid the foundation for in-depth discipleship and taught of life in Jesus and learning to hear the Holy Spirit. Over the past century, the study of spiritual formation and development has seen a great resurgence as Christians from all denominations—Protestants and Catholics alike—have sought a richer, deeper relationship with God that rises above denominational spirituality. Even in Restoration churches, including the International Church of Christ, many are discovering the benefits of the spiritual disciplines and spiritual formation.

---

46. Bernard of Clairvaux, *The Love of God.*

In 1978, Scott Peck wrote a classic, *A Road Less Traveled,* which fueled interest in life's spiritual journey among both the religious and irreligious. Richard Foster's Celebration of Discipline and Dallas Willard's *Spirit of the Disciplines* fueled the growing interest in Christian spirituality through their deep spiritual teaching. In the early 1980s, James Fowler, an American theologian and professor of human development, presented a modern understanding of spiritual development in the stages of faith. Today there are many great models to study and understand the stages of our spiritual development. Janet Hagberg and Robert A. Guelich have written what is considered by many the standard model of spiritual development in their book *The Critical Journey: Stages in the Life of Faith.* Great spiritual guides such as Richard Foster, Ronald Rolheiser, Richard Rohr, David Brennan, Dallas Willard, Ruth Haley Barton, and many more are trailblazing our understanding of the way we grow in Christ. Their discoveries have ignited a spiritual awareness that is authentic in the true biblical sense. Many fellowships, including our own, have underappreciated and ignored the Holy Spirit's role in our development. The models these leaders have developed over the centuries offer helpful and important insights into our spiritual journey.

The following are some of the universal and common stages and a brief description of each. Understanding these stages requires greater attention and time than one chapter allows. A brief explanation must suffice for now.

Spiritual Stages of Life

Stage 1 (Preliminary Stage): Chaos

The earliest stage is typically a sort of chaotic, wild, and open stage in which there is an absence of direction, order, and rules. This is comparable to the preschool years in human development. A child has no set schedule and very few rules or expectations to live by. This is the pre-Christian life. Such a person has no authentic or established religion. At this stage, a person might make up their religion as they go through life from the smorgasbord of philosophies, religions, and movies they have encountered. There is no clear expectation of discipline, denial, or beliefs, beyond opinions and feelings that fluctuate and are influenced easily. No standard of life has been adopted yet. Their universe is still empty and void, and their hallmark is ignorance.

Stage 2 (Earliest Stage): Conversion

In this stage, a person has a religious experience, an encounter with God, and they join the faith. Hagberg and Guelich call this time the recognition of God. At this point, a person has a major spiritual event that disrupts their world, and they discover God. Everything is turned upside down and suddenly God/Jesus is the excitement and center of their life. They are overwhelmed with a sense of amazement and spiritual hunger. Enthusiasm and joy are at a peak in this stage. Life is full of potential, and Christianity is filled with awe and wonder.

Stage 3: Conformity

Stage three entails adopting and embracing the new Christian life. At this point in a person's spiritual journey, everything focuses on conforming to the group. The church becomes our family, and we strive to fit in and be part of the community. We learn to seek the kingdom first and adopt the church's culture as our own. In the ICOC, we acquire the lingo, and everything is "awesome." Developmentally, this is like a child who enters school and suddenly has to learn rules and norms to adopt and perform. A child learns to raise their hand when they desire to speak and stand in line and wait their turn. These are some of the important rules of society that allow it to work. Similarly, these social and cultural rules in the church help us grow in Christ and in the community of faith.

We learn not only a new vocabulary, but also about dating, spiritual friendships, having quiet times, and even the way to pray, as well as many other things that help us take our first steps of life in Jesus. We are enculturated and indoctrinated into the church. The proverbial "I" becomes part of the "we" and "us" of the fellowship. We are proud to be part of the holy nation, the royal priesthood, the people of God. It is a time of simple, childlike faith full of naïveté, but we are filled with the joy of our faith. The kingdom of God is an exciting, daily discovery.

Stage 4: Quality

At this point, we begin to achieve spiritual proficiency in being contributing members of the church. We know what and how to practice the basic requirements of life in Christ. We begin to excel in different aspects of a disciple's life. We know the way to have a good quiet time, share our faith, and study our Bibles. Some of us begin to excel in diverse areas of life in Christ, bearing fruit, growing in our Bible knowledge, even teaching or preaching. Some stand out as leaders or proficient speakers who encourage everyone with their gifts. *The Critical Journey*[47] refers to this as the productive stage of spirituality. We fill our lives with fruitful labor and delight in it.

Stage 5: Questioning

At some point along the path, after years of faithful service, many experience a quiet but growing disturbance in their faith. This stage is marked by internal questions that surface gradually. Questions about the Bible, the church, the leadership, or our role in the fellowship become of primary importance. We begin to dissect or deconstruct in our minds and hearts all that we once accepted fully and believed without question. As we come to realize, know, and experience the church's weaknesses and the culture's flaws, we cannot help but wonder about it all. Ultimately, everyone experiences this stage to different degrees and in different ways.

Further, it is not uncommon to experience this stage several times in life. With respect to developmental stages, this is adolescence. Ask any preteen or teen's parent and they can attest to the challenge of this period of life. Suddenly, everything is questioned, including parental authority and family rules and culture. Parents often struggle to handle adolescents in the family. Similarly,

---

47. Janet O. Hagberg and Robert A. Guelich, *The Critical Journey: Stages in the Life of Faith* (Salem, WI: Sheffield, 2005).

many churches' leaders struggle to cope with spiritual adolescence. Sometimes entire groups of people reach this stage together, and the church becomes deconstructed. As difficult as this stage may be, it is an essential one on the path to maturity. For some, this is the stage in which faith moves from hopeful positivity to authentic trust in the Lord. At other times, deeper faith and richer love are discovered, rooted, and established as unconditional only through questions and testing. In this way, the difficult child who is loved unconditionally comes to know and appreciate unconditional love. This is certainly the most trying of the spiritual stages. Many fall away, and many mishandle this stage of spiritual formation. Many refer to this stage as "the wall" or even "a wall" because it can occur multiple times in a person's life. Handled spiritually, these difficult times in life make us far stronger as they purify and refine our faith.[48]

Stage 6: Conviction

When a person is able to keep their eyes on Jesus and see God's hand in the challenges they face, they are ushered into a mature faith. A person who works through their questions rarely finds answers to them all. In their quest for answers, they realize that there are some good answers to many of their questions, but there are also some mysteries that God will not reveal to us. We realize that God does not answer to us; rather, we answer to him. However, the search for answers often reveals God's goodness and brilliance. Even when one is coping with problems in the church, one cannot escape the fact that the church is God's design and Jesus' bride. Despite all its flaws, the church provides the perfect place to learn to be like Jesus. It is a spiritual petri dish in which spirituality can grow.

Unlike the naiveté of people in stages 3 and 4, in this stage we see all the problems and weaknesses in the church, yet we can see God's hand in each of them. It is in this experiential knowledge that we choose to love, forgive, act in mercy, and walk in deep-root-

---

48. "These have come so that the proven genuineness of your faith—of greater worth than gold, which perishes even though refined by fire—may result in praise, glory and honor when Jesus Christ is revealed" (1 Peter 1:7).

ed faith. We begin to understand that love truly covers a multitude of sins. Grace and mercy abound as our faith deepens in our knowledge of God.

Stage 7: Convergence

This is the truly great stage where all that we have learned appears to come together in him. Few people ever reach this stage of spirituality. Truth, love, and the Holy Spirit dominate this stage. The truth we have learned about ourselves becomes the reality in which we live. The truth of our weakness, sinfulness, and limitations has driven us to profound dependence on God through the Holy Spirit, while the truth of God's goodness, mercy, and love for us and all humans establishes a profound sense of peace, security, and mercy. God's love fills us as a reservoir from which we can love, forgive, and serve others freely. The spiritual depth we have developed through years of obedience and practice empower us to overcome fear and temptation, not by our strength, but his. We can be set free and healed from our sins and our neighbors' sins.

At this stage we learn the way of Jesus and choose to be empowered by sails, not oars. The fruit of the spirit—love, joy, peace, patience, kindness, and self-control—becomes increasingly evident in every area of our lives. We discover the secret of being content in all situations, even while in this world with all its troubles and pains. We learn to walk in the knowledge of Christ and live led by his Spirit. His yoke is easy and his burden light while we discover *shalom.* In this final stage, everything we have learned, experienced, and practiced coalesces, and we learn to be our true selves made in the image of God. We have relinquished fear and worry about our egos and selves and delight in God's love. We eagerly anticipate and are ready for the final stage of complete oneness with our Creator.

> *His divine power has given us everything we need for a godly life through our knowledge of him who called us by his own glory and goodness. Through these he has given us his very great and precious promises, so that through them you may participate in the divine nature, having escaped the corruption in the world caused by evil desires.*

For this very reason, make every effort to add to your faith goodness; and to goodness, knowledge. (2 Peter 1:3–5)

The spiritual journey is a marvelous voyage of transformation filled with excitement and challenge. We mature and make important changes on this journey that move us forward in Christ from death to life. Conversion begins when we come to faith and receive baptism, but it takes a lifetime to run its course fully in our souls. Our Father in heaven provides for us everything we need for the journey and the great transition. We are given Scripture, mentors, companions, examples, and particularly the Holy Spirit to guide us along the way. Amazingly, we are invited to participate in the divine nature! We are called to live as we were created to be, in the *imago Dei,* or image of God.

In this lifelong process, we are transformed from filled with fear to filled with faith, from self-centeredness and selfishness to love and service. We move from shame and guilt to freedom and confidence. Fear is truly the beginning of wisdom,[49] but it is love that compels us to the very end. We move from a religion of rules to a love relationship with the divine and learn to love each other. Our Christianity shifts from doing more to being more. We are transformed with ever-increasing glory into his likeness. Unlike Moses, whose glory was fading, ours increases with time and permanence.[50]

As we evolve spiritually, we shine brighter and brighter still. As we develop in Christ, the spiritual journey demands us to surrender ourselves and allow God to transform our minds. This process is the very reason spiritual disciplines were established and have been practiced for centuries. In them we learn to be still and know God. In them we make space for God in our hearts, minds, and souls. We learn to listen for God's gentle whisper.

We have much to say about this, but it is hard to make it clear to you because you no longer try to understand. In fact, though by this time you ought to be teachers, you need someone to teach you the elementary truths of God's

---

49. "The fear of the Lord is the beginning of wisdom, and knowledge of the Holy One is understanding" (Proverbs 9:10).

word all over again. You need milk, not solid food! Anyone who lives on milk, being still an infant, is not acquainted with the teaching about righteousness. But solid food is for the mature, who by constant use have trained themselves to distinguish good from evil. (Hebrews 5:11–14)

Spiritual development is not something that should be left to chance or ignored. Being a church member for many years does not guarantee maturity, it only guarantees becoming old. We who have spent our lives in faithful service, sacrificing so much, certainly do not wish to end by becoming old wineskins. Our spiritual development is a vital part of our Christianity and key to being faithful till the end. The Hebrew writer warns us all to mature and not become stagnant. It is our nature to plateau and rest on our early achievements. We must be aware, push ourselves forward, and learn to rely on the Holy Spirit.

There are many great discoveries to be realized as long as we have breath in our lungs. Without the knowledge of the Lord and guidance from the Holy Spirit, the Christian life can be heavy and burdensome rather than light and easy as Jesus promised. Much of my Christian life, as victory filled as it has been, was anything but light and easy.[51] Jesus invites us to be yoked with him so that he can give us rest and we may experience the light burden and easy yoke. Jesus invites us to share in his glory![52] On a personal note, I will soon turn forty years old in the faith. Happily, I consider this the most wonderful time of my Christian life, and I have been blessed to experience many exciting adventures in the Lord. I cannot wait to see what is ahead as I strive and hope to mature even to stage 7. I am learning to live with Jesus and walk in the Holy Spirit in ways previously unimagined. I love where Jesus is leading me.

---

50. "And we all, who with unveiled faces contemplate the Lord's glory, are being transformed into his image with ever-increasing glory, which comes from the Lord, who is the Spirit" (2 Corinthians 3:18).

51. "Come to me, all you who are weary and burdened, and I will give you rest. Take my yoke upon you and learn from me, for I am gentle and humble in heart, and you will find rest for your souls. For my yoke is easy and my burden is light" (Matthew 11:28–30).

52. "He called you to this through our gospel, that you might share in the glory of our Lord Jesus Christ" (2 Thessalonians 2:14).

For this very reason, make every effort to add to your faith goodness; and to goodness, knowledge; and to knowledge, self-control; and to self-control, perseverance; and to perseverance, godliness; and to godliness, mutual affection; and to mutual affection, love. For if you possess these qualities in increasing measure, they will keep you from being ineffective and unproductive in your knowledge of our Lord Jesus Christ. (2 Peter 1:5–8)

We are all in need of the Lord's guidance throughout our entire Christian life. This is the great adventure. We are meant to experience the Lord with ever-increasing glory. As we grow older in the faith, we must nourish our souls with solid food, not milk. From womb to tomb, we need the Lord and his increasing guidance. Spiritual formation is the practice and discipline of living with intentional faith during every stage of life. Everyone is formed spiritually, but not everyone is formed well. The world is full of spiritual deformities. Even many churches are filled with poor theology that produces Christians who try to white-knuckle their way into heaven. Too many churches rely on guilt and shame to motivate their congregations. Guilt and shame are heavy burdens that exhaust the soul. Many of us resort to trying to earn our salvation rather than living in God's grace and mercy. The Bible teaches again and again that the cursed is any person who tries to save themselves through deeds or their own righteousness.[53] God has a far greater plan in mind for us through life in him. But we must learn how to "abide" in him during every stage in life.

Therefore, I urge you, brothers and sisters, in view of God's mercy, to offer your bodies as a living sacrifice, holy and pleasing to God—this is your true and proper worship. Do not conform to the pattern of this world, but be transformed by the renewing of your mind. Then you will be able to test and approve what God's will is—his good, pleasing, and perfect will. (Romans 12:1–2)

In today's church culture, we tend to place great emphasis on the early years of the spiritual journey and focus on conversion

---

53. "Cursed is the one who trusts in man, who draws strength from mere flesh" (Jeremiah 17:5).

and first principles, while we assume that disciples will continue to grow on their own. This is a serious mistake. Consequently, many Christians never reach spiritual maturity. Fewer than 25 percent[54] of those who begin a disciple's life reach stage 6 and far fewer stage 7. Too many church members are tired rather than inspired. Only the Holy Spirit can move them forward from survival to authentic revival. Similarly, churches around the world are lamenting the loss of younger generations. These new generations crave authentic spirituality that bypasses religiosity and empty tradition. We must remember and hold on to the promise that Jesus came to bring us "life...to the full," not routine and religiosity.

Maturity is the key to the "greater things"[55] that Jesus promised his disciples. In maturity we learn to let the Spirit guide us into love, joy, peace, patience, kindness, and self-control.[56] These attributes come not from willpower but directly from the Spirit through spirituality. There are many lessons that require a lifetime of training to live a God-centered life guided by the Holy Spirit. The spiritual disciplines are tools meant to train us for godliness with which we learn to discern the Holy Spirit and live aware of the presence of God. The Lord has many unclaimed promises available for those who are willing to pursue him in greater depth through all the stages of life and spirituality. Let us be aware of the journey, embrace it, and enjoy the adventure! Let us take the path that leads to becoming our true selves and live as we were created to be, in the image of God.

What you are is God's Gift to you,
What you become is your gift to GOD.   —Hans Urs Balthasar

With God's help...
I am becoming myself.   —Soren Kierkegaard

---

54. Andy Fleming, research and statistics of the ICOC.

55. "Very truly I tell you, whoever believes in me will do the works I have been doing, and they will do even greater things than these, because I am going to the Father" (John 14:12).

56. "But the fruit of the Spirit is love, joy, peace, forbearance, kindness, goodness, faithfulness, gentleness and self-control" (Galatians 5:22).

Resources

For more information about spiritual development and spiritual formation, please see my website, www.thewayofthepilgrim.com.

M. Robert Mulholland Jr. and Ruth Haley Barton, *Invitation to a Journey: A Road Map for Spiritual Formation* (Downers Grove, IL: InterVarsity, 2016).

Dallas Willard, *Renovation of the Heart: Putting on the Character of Christ* (Colorado Springs, CO: NavPress, 2002)

Henri J. M. Nouwen, *Spiritual Formation: Following the Movements of the Spirit* (New York, NY: HarperCollins, 2010).

CHAPTER TEN

Recovering from Spiritual Burnout: Combatting the Lies That Harm Our Hearts

Dr. Sean St. Jean, PhD

Sean has been a social worker and a counselor in private practice for the past twelve years. He holds both a bachelor's and clinical master's degree in social work from the University of British Columbia, as well as a PhD in social work and sociology. His research focus is on vicarious trauma and burnout among helping professionals. Sean has worked in child welfare as a child protection worker and then as a family preservation counselor. He also worked as a mental health case manager with WorkSafeBC, adjudicating occupational mental health claims. Currently he teaches graduate-level social work and is the Director of MSW Field Education at King University in Tennessee. In his counseling practice, Sean works with individuals struggling with anxiety and depression, posttraumatic and occupational stress, burnout, and relationship issues using cognitive, psychodynamic, and faith-based approaches. Sean and his wife, Erin, and their three children currently live in British Columbia and are active members of the church in Vancouver.

Young love is a rare and precious thing. What makes it even better is when we see God's hand working through it. I don't often speak of mystical matters, but there is a single event in my life that I would call a bona fide miracle. When I was in my mid-twenties I attended my cousin's wedding in a tiny town in rural British Columbia, Canada. I remember somberly leaving the reception hall, pacing in the dark along the sandy shore of a random lake. I was lonely. I deeply longed for someone to share my life with. Standing at the still water's edge for a long while, I prayed to God that he would find me a wife. As I prayed, I stared across the lake at a hill, the lights of the houses upon it flickering in the waning summer warmth. I wasn't in on the joke yet.

I am sure that God and his angels were smiling as I prayed. You see, as I begged God to bring a marriage partner into my life, I just happened to be staring at the very hill my future wife grew up on. Understand that I had never been to this out-of-the-way town. I had never seen this hill. I didn't know it at the time, but God had a plan.

Our love grew quickly and intensely. Everything in our relationship seemed impossibly easy, and I felt as though my feet never touched the ground the entire time we were dating. Not long after, we were married on that very same hill, and most of our church made the five-hour trek there to celebrate with us.

I also experienced a different sort of young love in those days, a spiritual passion that seemed almost effortless. I had been leading a small campus ministry on a mission team to Edmonton, Alberta. Those were the days of massive on-campus evangelism campaigns and reams of Bible studies with students who were seeking God. I don't remember much about the college classes I took, but I do remember teaching the word of God study over and over again to willing students at the campus cafeteria. I recall feeling a deep sense of meaning and purpose as souls were being saved and people's lives were being forever changed. I felt supremely effective, like God and I had a solid working relationship. Yes, those were the glory days.

Yet what does all of this have to do with spiritual burnout? You probably get the sense that what made my fledgling relationship with my eventual wife so special was the fact that it was fleeting. We can only be "new" in our relationship once, and no other stage has quite the same magic. When we are in love, we often love who we are in the relationship. Likewise, you may recall your own feelings of young and zealous faith; the fresh and uncomplicated satisfaction of knowing you were actively loving Jesus and making a difference in the world. When we partner with God in this way, we often love who we are in that relationship too.

Burnout might be described as the loss of that young love.

Christina Maslach, the "mother" of secular burnout research, defines the phenomenon of burnout as the long-term response to chronic stressors, usually in our work. Think of your initial passion giving way to endless paperwork and impossible job demands. The blush has come off the rose. The meaning we longed to feel in our work has disappointingly evaporated.

Maslach breaks the concept of burnout down into three parts: overwhelming emotional exhaustion, feelings of cynicism or detachment, and a sense of ineffectiveness or lack of accomplishment. My doctoral research was about how these factors negatively affect helping professionals: social workers, nurses, first responders, and the like. What I have discovered is that these vocational concepts apply to our spiritual lives as well. We will cover these three dimensions slowly over the course of this chapter.

Spiritual burnout is akin to occupational burnout in that it shares many of the same toxic elements. As a therapist, I can tell you that after the "honeymoon period" ends, marriages often face a myriad of challenges. Difficulties raising children, financial woes, relational frustrations, and differences in worldviews can eventually rob us of that "early love" we had for our spouse. In the same way, the joy of our young faith can fall victim to overwhelming ministry demands, irritating disputes with other Christians, and various disappointments or frustrations. Over time, these contribute to a deluge of emotional exhaustion or cynicism, or a sense of disillusionment, as well as feelings of ineffectiveness in the church.

Overwhelming Emotional Exhaustion

We do not want you to be uninformed, brothers and sisters, about the troubles we experienced in the province of Asia. We were under great pressure, far beyond our ability to endure, so that we despaired of life itself. (1 Corinthians 1:8)

We get the sense here that whatever trials Paul went through had outstripped his emotional capacities. They overpowered his ability to cope. And let's face it: both then and now, our church is an intense place. The assembly of believers is both a wonderful blessing and a bit overwhelming at times. It reminds me of the scripture that tells us to "rejoice with those who rejoice; mourn with those who mourn" (Romans 12:15). Most of us are collectively swayed, for better or worse, by the disciples around us, and we tend to be deeply affected by "how the church is doing."

The fellowship can also be both a concentrator and amplifier of emotions. For example, when a tragedy happens in the life of a disciple, word quickly spreads (often in vivid detail) about the incident. We all feel it. Likewise, as we go through our own struggles, advice and "support" can be multiplied and pressurized by many voices to the degree that it can feel more hurtful than helpful. A more lighthearted example I have personally experienced is of being asked by dozens of people, "So, when are you going to start dating?" When Erin and I did start dating, perhaps thirty or forty people in the congregation immediately asked me, "When are you going to get married?" Soon after the wedding, a veritable parade of disciples asked me, "So, when are you going to have your first child?" It was as though my brothers and sisters saw it as their solemn duty to push us forward in life!

Our hearts can also suffer because of the negative sentiments that circulate around the church, like "The church isn't doing well spiritually" or "We don't have the zeal for the lost that we used to have." Criticisms like "The minister is out of touch with the congregation" or "The leadership has a hidden agenda" can swirl through the body of believers, seeding cynicism and disillusionment in our hearts. Some of us have even endured spiritual abuse and hurts from the past that have made connecting with God and other disciples an uphill battle. Being exposed to these words, challenges, struggles, and difficult memories as they continually wash over us can lead to a sense of utter exhaustion. It can feel as though we can't get our spiritual motor running in spite of our best efforts. More on this in the next section.

When we feel like we are emotionally exhausted in our local ministry, it might be a simple matter of stepping back, of taking a sabbath day or a vacation or laying aside some of our church responsibilities for a season. Indeed, the other chapters in this book are designed to help with that. I often ask my counseling clients to measure the severity of their exhaustion by saying, "How much rest or downtime do you think you would need before you could come back feeling refreshed and energized? Three days? Three weeks? Three months? Dare I say three years?" The answer to that question provides good data about how much a person has been affected by burnout and the scale of what they might need to recover.

We aren't done with burnout yet. It is probably fair to say that everyone gets really tired on occasion because of the busyness of church commitments. What pushes simple exhaustion into the "burnout zone" are Maslach's other two elements, to be covered next.

Cynicism, Disillusionment, and Detachment

"You will not certainly die," the serpent said to the woman. "For God knows that when you eat from it your eyes will be opened, and you will be like God, knowing good and evil." (Genesis 3:4–5)

It might be said that Satan's primary strategy is to push a wedge between us and God. And he does this primarily by undermining God's motives and encouraging cynicism. Cynicism is a darkening of one's worldview that happens when people are exposed to evil, either directly or through the stories they hear from others. This causes us to question our fundamental beliefs about the nature of the world. In my field we call this "vicarious trauma"; a profound shift in the way helping professionals (like social workers, nurses, or first responders) see the world that occurs when they are deluged by the repeated traumatic narratives shared by clients. Christians, too, can be highly susceptible to an undercurrent of negative or undermining messages that can run through a congregation. Our belief about the goodness of God, the hope we have of heaven, and views about our purpose in the world can be shattered if those toxic messages take root (Hebrews 12:15).

Disillusionment is cynicism's evil cousin. It describes feelings of deep disappointment that can settle into our hearts when we realize (or falsely believe) that a wonderful thing isn't actually as good as we once thought it was. Think of Peter after he betrayed Jesus and then lost him to the cross. I can imagine him murmuring, "I guess I'd better go back to my nets. This Messiah thing was too good to be true." In the same way, we can look back at the trajectory of our family of churches and quietly say to ourselves, "I guess God wasn't with us after all" or "All my work for God was in vain." These sentiments might never be spoken aloud, but they can still be very destructive to our faith if they take root inside us. They also conceal sinister lies that Satan uses to deceive us into giving up our inheritance. More to follow on that.

What makes cynicism and disillusionment so dangerous is that they cause our hearts to harden. What's more, these evil cousins can cause us to distance ourselves from God and other Christians (Hebrews 3:12–14). They are like festering wounds that make the initial injury worse. In fact, the path that leads us to spiritual harm is both predictable and right out of Satan's playbook: enduring an overload of stressful church commitments over time combined with a barrage of disheartening whispers (created within us or received from others) gives rise to cynicism if we believe those lies. Detachment from God and our fellow believers is Satan's endgame. This is his most sinister ambition. But there is still one more crucial aspect of spiritual burnout. It is the final nail in our spiritual coffins.

Personal Ineffectiveness

> I planted the seed, Apollos watered it, but God has been making it grow. So neither the one who plants nor the one who waters is anything, but only God, who makes things grow. (1 Corinthians 3:6–7)

It is in our nature to crave success, however we might define it. As the expression goes, "To a carpenter, every problem is a nail and every solution is a hammer." Doctors want to heal patients. Teachers want to develop their students' minds. Runners want to win the race or achieve their personal best time. For Christians in our family of churches, the markers of success have traditionally come in the form of baptisms, growing the church, increasing our giving (financially or through service), and pursuing a meaningful relationship with God. The problem is when these success markers become a precondition to our sense of self-worth and worthiness before God. The matter is made worse when our goals are incorrectly conceived in the first place.

What I have described relates to the third main element of burnout, which is having a sense of what clinicians might call low self-efficacy. That's just a fancy way of saying that we don't have much faith or confidence in our ability to be victorious over something. When we have a track record of not achieving our spiritual goals, our view of ourselves can become cynical or hopeless. This process demotivates us; we often stop trying because "What's the point?" This leads to a downward spiral of low self-esteem and learned helplessness as our lack of effort gives rise to a self-fulfilling prophesy of sorts. This might look like self-judgment about our personal righteousness, our closeness with God, our "personal fruitfulness" or evangelism goals, or even our reputation in the church.

This struggle is certainly one I have had at times. I remember as a young Christian feeling as though we were the church who "got it." We were the ones who "made it happen" by actively saving souls and winning the world for Christ. I was proud of our identity as a movement.

Back then, Saturday date nights were routinely interrupted so that we could call in our "commitments" (the people we were bringing to church) to our ministry leaders. During the Sunday service, every visitor was accounted for, and we made sure we all connected with whoever came out. The minister would almost always say at some point during his sermon, "If you would like to learn more about [that day's topic], please turn to the person who brought you out today and ask them to study the Bible with you." We carefully tracked who was coming to church, who was studying the Bible, what study they were on, and what they needed to do to become Christians. We were a well-oiled machine, amazing and terrifying at the same time. During those years, I loved what we were doing, and perhaps more importantly, I loved who I was on this team of believers. My young self was sincerely proud of the ways I was contributing to this group of Christ-followers.

I'm not sure how that little narrative landed on you. Maybe you thought, "Ugh, we were so crazy back then" or perhaps, "Yes, I remember those days. They were glorious." I am frankly not here to do a postmortem on the way things used to be, though I now hold a more nuanced view of those days. The point is that for many of us who have been around for a while, our spiritual origin story set a very high bar for how we define "spiritual success," both individually and as a church.

Just as kids, careers, and the common worries of life may have gotten in the way of the passion we had as newlyweds, I have no doubt that those very same trials have also affected our ability to meet our original expectations for spiritual performance. Speaking for myself, it has never been more difficult to carve out time for Bible study, prayer, and evangelism than it is today, in the midst of kid and teen chaos, career obligations, and other church commitments.

On a collective level, we might also feel unsupported when we, say, bring a friend out to church. Our refrain may be, *"What's the point of inviting people? No one even says 'hi' to my visitors anymore."* Many of us are still grieving not only the loss of a dream and our spiritual expectations, but a loss of our collective spiritual identity as well.

Witch's Brew

Metanoia, the Greek word for mind change, or repentance, in the New Testament, has been said to refer to a radical realignment of our worldview with God's view of the world as his word does its work in our hearts. Yet Satan aims for precisely the opposite. He seeks to kill and destroy (John 10:10); he is a ruthless murderer, his favorite murder weapon being deception (John 8:44). The devil's modus operandi is to push us off a philosophical and spiritual ledge through deceptions, half-truths, and confusion.

When Maslach's three burnout elements—emotional exhaustion, disillusionment, and feelings of personal failure—emulsify over time, they form a toxic cocktail that harms us spiritually. Spiritual burnout is different from straightforward exhaustion because it is more than just extreme tiredness; it is a treacherous shift in the way we view reality. It is a gangrene that destroys the infected tissue of our hearts. Like the witch in Snow White, the devil feeds us this poison apple to put us into a deep sleep, ending our spiritual lives.

So, what are we to do? The second half of the chapter provides strategies for countering this faith-stealing trifecta. These are not exhaustive solutions, but they are designed to provide you with a compass reading as you journey toward spiritual wholeness. This is a both a broad and nuanced topic, tailored for those within our family of churches. Because of this, I am presenting only a few foundational ideas in each category.

Working Through Spiritual Burnout

1. Recovering from Emotional Exhaustion

> *"Come to me, all you who are weary and burdened, and I will give you rest. Take my yoke upon you and learn from me, for I am gentle and humble in heart, and you will find rest for your souls. For my yoke is easy and my burden is light."* (Matthew 11:28–30)

Jesus' (surprising) example

How do we start taking forward steps to address emotional exhaustion? While the work of Satan may sound dire (and it is!), Jesus provides comfort in the storm and is a lamp for our feet (Psalm 119:105). But maybe not quite as we imagine. I resolutely believe that following Jesus is always the solution, even if (especially if) you are on the floor, spiritually. In therapy we often say, "If trying harder isn't working, maybe you could try differently." We also say that "the definition of insanity is doing the same thing over and over again, expecting a different result." In keeping with this idea, I would invite you to consider a few new colors I am adding to the palette as we paint this portrait of Jesus. Now, these aren't my colors; they have actually been sitting in the box all along.

As a God-seeker and a baby Christian, I relished my church's recasting of the King of kings. I had grown tired of the sad, sopping, pleading, irrelevant Jesus I grew up with. I think you know what I'm talking about. My eighteen-year-old self was elated when the men who studied the Bible with me painted over the dripping wet, Shakespearean-accented Jesus and started applying new colors to the canvas. Instead, the brothers sketched out a powerful, resolute, confident Jesus who was unaffected by his enemies and who dominated every circumstance. He was loving, yes, but he was always also squarely in control. He was Superman. He was William Wallace in Braveheart. He left it all on the field. And in the end, he died a hero's death, only to ultimately conquer death itself. And based on that painting, I was all in.

However, as the years went by, I realized that this portrait of Jesus was actually missing a few crucial pigments. And as I wrestled with my own nagging weaknesses, shattered dreams, and doubts about my faith, I realized that even "Braveheart Jesus" fell short. He was an untouchable superhero caricature that I worshipped, rather than the also-human savior who was tempted in every way and made perfect through suffering. Had I overemphasized the divinity of Jesus, and in doing so neglected his humanity—the part that was just like me? I realized that in order to be led through spiritual brokenness, I would need to follow a God who could relate to my fallen human nature.

So let me throw this color into the mix: Jesus wasn't a martyr.

I know, I know, this is sacrilege, right? Let me affirm that I believe that Christ died for my sins on the cross. In fact, this is at the center of my faith. What I mean is that Jesus had a sense of unconditional permission to enjoy his life. To him, life was its own end; both in the temporal and eternal sense. The point is often made that Jesus *was only born so that he could die for us.* Over the years we have emphasized Jesus' mission, his relentlessness, and his sacrifice. And these are deeply important. But have you ever considered all the ways that Jesus simply met his own needs? They tend to go unnoticed because they were simply the background of his life. Here is a short list:

- Jesus slept on a boat while a violent storm was raging and his disciples were freaking out. (Mark 4:38)
- Jesus was called a glutton and a drunkard, suggesting he enjoyed his social life. (Luke 7:34)
- Jesus routinely left the crowds to take time away. (Luke 4:1–2; Mark 6:31; Matthew 14:13; Luke 6:12, 5:16)
- Jesus wept. (John 11:35)
- Jesus acknowledged when he "wasn't okay." (Matthew 26:38–39)

One of the things that weary disciples seek from me in therapy sessions is permission to rest. Their views of discipleship have been partially informed by the Scriptures and partially informed by the command, example, and inference of *people*. That is, they live (consciously or unconsciously) by a cultural hermeneutic; a lens through which they view God's expectations.

As we walk through our journey of recovery from spiritual burnout, let's keep the following in mind: it is not a sin to take care of yourself. In fact, I believe that it is a sin not to. When we work ourselves to the bone, we transgress against God's design for our lives. Jesus leads the way in this. Let us also obey Jesus' example of self-care just as we seek to obey his call to sacrifice and self-denial.

Shift your environment

Imagine waking up to near silence. There are no chimes, apps, or TV sounds. There is no traffic. No background music. No mechanical anything. The near silence allows a different set of sounds to emerge. Wind through the trees. Birds chirping in the distance. Laughter of children. The sound of our own breath.

I know you just took a deep breath; I did. Let's keep using our imagination. There are no cars. There's no electricity. No email. No podcasts. No smartphones. All of life is designed around basic human needs. People live cloistered together rather than in isolation. Distances are based on how far people's feet can take them. There are no parking lots.

Everything is slow. Gloriously slow. The earth's natural cycles determine when we go to sleep and when we wake up. There is no concern about "blue light" at 1:00 am. When darkness begins to fall, your time is up. The day is over! Those same cycles determine when we plant and when we harvest. God is fully in charge of the rhythms of life. During certain seasons, everyone is out in the fields, regardless of their trade. The harvest is plentiful, but the workers are few. During the winter season, there is relatively little to do except rest and connect. People are rarely in a rush. Company is welcome. People are the most important thing.

This was the everyday backdrop of Jesus' life.

I humbly submit that our modern lives look nothing like this. We have been stressed to the max by, among other things, our own ingenuity. Every aspect of life is now ultra-refined. Our overwhelming wealth and "success" have led to a crisis of busy. We have become addicted to our own stress hormones. And this is 100 percent true for our life inside the church as well. The only question I want to ask you is this: Could your ability to more richly follow Jesus come not from pulling yourself up by your own bootstraps, but instead from shifting your environment to look more like the one I just described?

Now, I am not saying that the days of Jesus represented some kind of utopian ideal. Nor am I advocating a return to a luddite mode of existence. I'm not a hippie. I like my car and my laptop and the internet and anesthetic at the dentist and antiperspirant and my glasses. I am merely pointing out that the world Jesus walked in was optimized for human beings. Perhaps rather than trying harder, we need to try differently. Maybe if we work to recreate our environment, that more nurturing environment will, in turn, recreate us.

The things we own, own us back. The tools we use, use us too. Peter warns that people are slaves to whatever has mastered them (2 Peter 2:19). Ask yourself this: Do you control your schedule, or does your schedule control you? I won't cover the points already made elsewhere in this book, except to say that over time, the things we commit to on our calendar eventually characterize our life. Be careful what you say yes to; we have found crafty ways to bypass God's rhythms. When God created the earth with those cycles and patterns, he had our well-being in mind. I contend that going back to those God-given cycles, even in part, will foster some of the recovery from exhaustion we so desperately need.

When it comes to roles in the church, my wife and I strive to put down boundaries. We say "no" far more than we say "yes" to requests. It can be tempting to commit oneself because it feels good to be asked and we don't want to let our church family down. I have also noticed that an ego-stroke is all it takes for me to buy in (yes, I am prideful!). But saying no isn't selfish. In fact, it is crucial to surviving the spiritual battle. We typically require forty-eight hours' notice for even "quick favors," a week or more for slightly larger things (like speaking at a Sunday service), and months to prayerfully decide whether to take on an ongoing or more substantial role. We also avoid committing to a bigger thing without checking in with each other first. These are tactical steps, designed to afford us the margin we need to walk more mindfully through our weeks.

I recently challenged a burned-out brother to remove a full 50 percent of his church commitments. I convinced him that the remaining 50 percent would be a healthy 100 percent for most people! What about you? What would it take for you to enjoy a more human-level, God's-limit-respecting pace in your life? What would you need to say "no" to in order to create some healthy margins in your week? To some, cutting back our commitments to the church may sound like a loss. Yet I am convinced that in most cases, taking that step back will actually carry us two steps forward. As the marines say, "Slow is smooth, and smooth is fast."

2. Recovering from Cynicism and Disillusionment

> *I am afraid that just as Eve was deceived by the serpent's cunning, your minds may somehow be led astray from your sincere and pure devotion to Christ. (2 Corinthians 11:3)*

Look for the wound
How do we recover from wounds to our heart? Crucially, we must recognize that cynicism is a form of spiritual trauma that

requires healing in the first place. Trauma damages us in a way that impedes normal functioning of the body, mind, and spirit. Consider the difference between being exhausted after a training run versus spraining an ankle on that run. Tiredness doesn't mean your legs are broken. You just need rest and then you will be ready to run again. A sprained ankle is a much different thing in that the tissue is damaged. That's trauma. In those cases, you probably need to stay off your foot for a few weeks before slowly putting weight on it again. In the case of a severe injury, you might even discover that you can never run in quite the same way you once did.

Spiritual trauma is much the same, except that instead of an ankle, what gets wounded is our belief system and motivations. Our views of God, the church, and ourselves can be skewed by Satan, opening the door to sin and disconnection. Those evil cousins, cynicism and disillusionment, represent damaged faith in God's portrayal of the world. Remember how the serpent got to Eve? He attacked her heart by creating disillusionment within her about God. He replaced the truth (God has my best interests in mind, so I should trust his rules) with a lie (God is holding his knowledge back from me because he doesn't want to share his power. I had better put my own interests first so I don't miss out).

This fundamental falsehood was the wedge in the door that enabled every other bad thing that followed in Eve's life. This lie had the cascading effect of causing Eve to doubt God's goodness, to act in her own perceived self-interest, to violate God's command, to be flooded with shame and guilt, and to lose her home in the garden. We have seen a similar dynamic in recent years as people have "deconstructed" their faith. But let's just call this what it is: destruction. There is a big difference between faithfully rethinking, reworking, or renovating our spiritual home versus taking a wrecking ball to our faith and running from the garden.

Many of us carry the wound of cynicism and are figuratively "outside the garden walls." Maybe we struggle to give our hearts at church or to volunteer. Perhaps we carry bitterness toward other church members and avoid them in the fellowship. It might be said about us that "the worries of this life, the deceitfulness of wealth, and the desires for other things" have come in and choked the Word out of us (Mark 4:19) so that our faith cannot produce what it once did.

Do not be fooled. Cynicism can be very subtle at first. This is why it is called a "bitter root" (Hebrews 12:15). It starts small and is underground, but in the end cynicism can "defile many." Ask God to reveal your heart to you. As David said in Psalm 139, "Search me, God, and know my heart" (v. 23). One way to know if cynicism is present in your heart is to consider your response to sermons, to hearing other disciples' names, to ministry requests, or to visions cast by preachers. This will likely require you to carefully inspect the feeling that arises. Is it positive and welcoming or negative and rejecting? What is the message that enters your mind? Is it "This is awesome!" or "I am encouraged by this person/request/idea"? Or is it "This will never work" or "Here we go again" or "He has a secret agenda"? The latter feelings and mental statements are a warning sign that something is wrong. These might be fair self-statements based on evidence. There could also be a festering wound in our heart that we haven't discovered or acknowledged yet.

Look for the lie

What is the difference between prison bars and a sea wall? When does a barrier go from being protective to being restrictive? While many of our spiritual beliefs protect us and guide our lives in positive and godly ways, some of us live in mental prisons of our own making, with iron bars of thought and belief. Yet if we can shift our thinking and escape the lies of Satan that hold us captive, we can find freedom and peace.

I contend that some of us live in thought prisons. We can be paralyzed by a set of views, commands, and "shoulds" that lead to a sense of helplessness and hopelessness. To get our heads around this idea, consider what it's like to buy a used car online. You navigate to the car page and there are literally hundreds of thousands of cars for sale. It is a veritable blue ocean of vehicles to choose from. But maybe you really want a particular make and model, so you enter those search terms. This cuts the ocean down to a sea; still pretty big. But you want your car to be a certain year or newer. Your sea has now shrunk to a large lake. And you want the car to have less than 100,000 miles on it. The lake is now a pond. But you also want it to be accident-free and it needs to be blue, and you want to pay less than $5000 for it. The pond has dried up! There are no longer any choices. Why? You made too many demands and expected too much. Something had to give.

Satan wants us to have a works-based mentality. If you have found yourself bound by too many demands on your faith, your spiritual pond may have dried up. This happens when we treat the Scriptures primarily like a set of regulations or imperatives to be obeyed, rather than as the life-giving word of God. Satan would love for us to eventually see the Bible as a set of prison bars.

Most of my work as a counselor is helping people discover, weigh, and then challenge erroneous beliefs: cognitions that don't serve them and that give rise to damaging mindsets and attitudes. Just as God spoke the world into existence (Psalm 33:8–9), we too metaphorically speak our worlds into existence. Like the Pharisees, we can strain out a gnat and swallow a camel (Matthew 23:24). We often carry burdens that aren't ours to carry and at the same time neglect items that God thinks are crucial.

I believe that some people have left the church based on a lie. Perhaps they left because they believed the cost of following God was too high. But what if instead they fell prey to a lie of Satan: the lethal lie that they could never do enough to please God, so why even try? Perhaps this is the very thing that Jesus criticized the Pharisees for. In Matthew 23 Jesus said, "They tie up heavy, cumbersome loads and put them on other people's shoulders" (v. 4), and "You shut the door of the kingdom of heaven in people's faces. You yourselves do not enter, nor will you let in those enter who are trying to" (v. 13b). What if the lie of works-based righteousness was actually a spiritually lethal mind-poison cooked up by Satan to cause exhaustion and then cynicism (heart damage)?

Yet it's not only those who have left our family who have succumbed to this poison apple of works-based deception. How many of us who remain have bodies that are technically present, but with distant hearts? What if we've quietly said to ourselves, "What's the point?" and have checked out of the spiritual battle based on an errant view of how the battle is meant to be fought in the first place?

This reminds me of Shakespeare's Romeo and Juliet. In this tragic play, (spoiler alert!) both star-crossed lovers die by their own hands based on a lie. What makes this story tragic is that Romeo thinks his love is dead, though she is only under the spell of a powerful potion that has put her into a coma-like state. Filled with grief, he then drinks poison, ending his own life. Juliet awakens soon after to find her Romeo gone and uses his dagger to end her life. We wince at this narrative because it seems so senseless. Romeo acted on a wrong belief. The whispers of the devil can also be heard throughout this story.

Remember that Satan himself masquerades as an angel of light (2 Corinthians 11:14). He wants to throw us into confusion. This might be why such a large proportion of the New Testament is spent refuting false doctrine. Some wrong beliefs are especially sinister. They harm us because they cause our hearts to turn away from God and toward our fleshly desires, just as Eve did.

If our defense against the scourge of cynicism is to reject false beliefs, what is our offense? Let's revisit Satan's schemes. He attempted the same tricks with Jesus that he used on Eve, but this time, he turned up the heat. All it took for Eve to err was a single, well-delivered half-truth. I don't want to linger on the temptation of Jesus, except to say that the devil appealed to his flesh (turn these stones into bread), tried to create doubt about his identity as the Son of God (force God to prove that you are his Son by catching you), and tempted him with the riches, power, and glory of the material world (all this can be yours if you follow my principles). Each was a powerful lie leveled by Satan, and in each case, the antidote was the Scriptures.

How much more at risk than Jesus are we of falling victim to the same deceptions? Think about the subtle and even covert shifts in our worldview that can occur when we believe one of these falsehoods:

"God knows that when you eat [the fruit] you will be like God, knowing good and evil" (Genesis 3:4–5): God doesn't want to share his power. He is holding back what is rightfully yours. Therefore, you should act in your own self-interest. Eat what you want. Drink what you want. Engage in whatever pleasures you seek. These are lies.

"If You are the Son of God [in our case, child of God], tell these stones to become bread" (Matthew 4:3): As a son or daughter of God, you are entitled to take what you hunger for. In fact, the flesh matters more than the spirit. Your physical needs matter more than your spiritual needs. Lies! Can God really be trusted to reward you in the next life for the sacrifices you make in this world? This is a question concealing a lie.

"If You are the Son of God [child of God], throw Yourself down [the Bible says God will catch you]" (Matthew 4:6): Again, Satan is undermining the relationship. Casting doubt. God should give you tangible proof that he cares about you. In fact, the bad or painful things that have happened to you are proof that God is indifferent to your suffering. Sorry, that's a lie.

"All this I will give You [all of the kingdoms of the world] if you will bow down and worship me" (Matthew 4:9): This is the proverbial "deal with the devil." Doing things God's way will keep you poor and powerless. You can have it all. You can be whatever you want to be with no limits. This is your time; don't trust God's principles—they are designed to keep you small and irrelevant. Lies, lies, and more lies!

Against Satan's primary weapon (lies), Jesus' weapon was the truth. And there is no contest. The truth sets us free. When our hearts get twisted and hardened by cynicism and disillusionment, the truth of Scripture is vital medicine.

Yet my hope is that you do not pursue God's word in a legalistic way. Reading words on a page for a minimum required time is not the same as falling beautifully and desperately in love with God. I recommend that as you pick up your Bible anew, stick to the psalms for a while. Be indulgent. You are not picking up a burden, but rekindling romance with the love of your life. Do everything you need to do to foster your relationship with the Creator. Some people switch Bible versions. Others use an audio format. The goal here is to promote genuine interest and purify your heart and forge a new trust in the Almighty. That is the point. That is God's desire.

3. Recovering from the Blight of Perceived Personal Failures

> Then they asked him, "What must we do to do the works God requires?"
> Jesus answered, "The work of God is this: to believe in the one he has sent."
> (John 6:28–29)

The performance trap

In the 1999 movie *The Matrix,* the protagonist, Neo, fights to rescue people from a virtual mental prison that humans are trapped in. Neo's guide, Morpheus, explains that if you die in the matrix, you die in real life. He suggests that the mind "makes it real." I would humbly suggest that this is true for us as well. God created an objective world for us to live in—the real world—but we also live in a virtual, subjective world of our own making, which may or may not align with God's truth. As we have already covered, this subjectivity is Satan's playground. We have seen how the father of lies seeks to undermine our view of God's goodness, love, and trust-worthiness. Yet perhaps no greater threat exists than the lies we believe about our own worth and identity. If the devil can't convince you that God is unloving, maybe he can convince you that you are unlovable.

Having taught, trained, and counseled hundreds of helping professionals, the "master lie" that I have seen emerge time after time in them is "I am unworthy of love." This is a shame-filled statement that causes insecurity, guilt, fear, resentment, and eventually apathy as it short-circuits our emotional center. Indeed, there is good evidence that many people are drawn into the helping fields in an attempt to fill this void within themselves.

This master lie is revealed via the similar comments I hear, often through tears, in one-on-one therapy sessions. People make many detrimental self-statements like, "I am only worth as much as I produce" or "I have to do this perfectly or it is proof that I am unworthy" or "If I show vulnerability, I will be rejected" or "I must be able to fix other people's problems as proof of my worth" or "I must be the strong/dependable one—that is where my value comes from" or "If I show my wound I will be rejected." Do you see the theme here? Each one of these confessions contributes to the misbelief that "I must measure up in order to be worthy or loved."

These are extremely dangerous "I" statements. Sometimes they drive arrogant attitudes, when we are under the illusion that we are performing perfectly. But most of the time they create deadly doubt when we realize that we cannot possibly attain these stratospheric standards for acceptance. If your value as a human being is solely based on your ability to perform, you are on shaky ground indeed!

The world vigorously tries to counter this performance mindset with self-love messages like "You are enough" and "You are worthy." However, the challenge with this approach is that, at least according to the Bible, this is simply untrue. We are actually not enough, and we are certainly not worthy. And that is a good thing. What's more, this truth is at the heart of the gospel message. We will never be enough. We cannot build our own tower to heaven or climb our way over the pearly gates. We desperately need a Savior to rescue us. Because of this, these well-meaning but very untrue self-love messages leave us in an equally insecure position.

The good news is that you do not have to be worthy to have a seat at God's table. You only need to be willing to show up, imperfectly, and even inconsistently. It is not a requirement that you hit a certain human standard or achieve a certain goal. You just have to hang on until the credits roll. When we adopt a more realistic set of expectations (based on God's truth, rather than the devil's cynicism-causing lies) we can be freed from nagging self-criticism and self-doubt. Through God's grace we are liberated to just be; and with that being to give and love and, dare I say, adventure in this incredible universe with King Jesus presiding.

I am deliberately not giving "practicals" in this section. Maybe you don't need more action items. Maybe an endless stream of action items and expectations and goals and plans has been part of the problem. Performance-oriented people often grew up hearing the words, *"Don't just sit there. Do something!"* So for now I will simply say, *"Don't just do something. Sit there."* The work of God is to believe in the One he has sent (John 6:29).

Lower the bar for success

What binds together a cup of cold water, two copper coins, and a mustard seed? Two things come to mind: 1) They are each very small offerings, and 2) they are each cherished and honored by God. As we consider this third aspect of spiritual burnout, having a deep sense of spiritual ineffectiveness or failure, it is natural to ask, "How do I get my spiritual swagger back?" Okay, maybe nobody asks exactly that, but you get the point.

One of the main challenges of changing any particularly difficult habit, sin, or state is the overwhelm that comes from expecting ourselves to make "radical changes." And many of us have falsely believed that grand gestures are the only ones that matter to God. Think of the statements, "one-suitcase challenge" and "lightning repentance" and "go anywhere, do anything, give up everything for God." These can be both inspiring and overwhelming statements to our ears. They sound glorious and terrifying; like standing at Mount Everest basecamp nervously contemplating our ascent.

Having counseled many disciples over the years who have faced the scourge of spiritual burnout, I can attest to the fact that this kind of "grandiose" thinking usually doesn't help because it keeps us stuck. It keeps us staring up at Mount Everest and never taking the first step.

What tends to work better is to break your end goal down into small enough steps that you can find some beginning forward momentum. When considering the initial steps needed on a journey to heal your heart before God, what is your mustard seed? What are your two copper coins? One way to gauge how small that step should be is to sit with the idea of that first step in your mind and see how you feel. Are you resistant to it, or does it feel achievable? You will know the step is small enough when you no longer feel overwhelmed at the thought of taking it.

Do not underestimate how extremely low this bar might need to be. Practically, instead of saying, "I am going to start having quiet times for an hour every morning" say, "I am going to watch a five-minute Bible video on YouTube." Instead of saying, "I am going to have an all-night prayer," commit to "Each morning in the shower I will simply say, 'Good morning, God. Please be with me today.'" That's it. Don't try to do more. Let yourself heal. There is a time when you will probably need to put weight on that leg again, but not now. For now, you just need to stay off it until you're ready. Have patience and let God heal you.

The amazing thing about small steps is that momentum will build in its own time. Consider that the two copper coins are honored more by Jesus than the great gifts given by the wealthy (Mark 12:41–44). The cup of cold water produces a heavenly reward (Matthew 10:42). The mustard seed grows to become the largest of garden plants (Matthew 13:32) and also contains within it the power to move mountains (Matthew 17:20).

Conclusion

He who was seated on the throne said, "I am making everything new!" Then he said, "Write this down, for these words are trustworthy and true."

He said to me: "It is done. I am the Alpha and the Omega, the Beginning and the End. To the thirsty I will give water without cost from the spring of the water of life." (Revelation 21:5–6)

Perhaps the bad news is that when young love ages, it can never go back to that earlier state. The fledgling spark we once shared with our beloved must give way to something better. Something stronger. Mature love can be deep and rich and beautiful.

Likewise, we may also feel like we have been forced out of the garden of young faith. The pure and undivided devotion we felt toward God can give way to cynicism as Satan plays his long game. Furthermore, the idea of climbing back over those garden walls after becoming spiritually burned out sounds just about as easy as fighting an angel wielding a flaming sword. Thankfully, it is a part of God's design to have us leave our naïve ways behind (Hebrews 5:12) and move on to maturity. Let us not allow grief about what once was to sabotage the better spiritual treasures that lay ahead for us.

The truth is, we do get to reenter the garden. We will be permitted to reach out our hand and eat from the Tree of Life. Amazingly, at the end of time and when all is said and done, the garden that we inherit will have grown into a great city. We are receiving an unshakable kingdom from a God who is a consuming fire. As we seek to recover from the icy clutches of spiritual burnout, may we allow God to set our hearts aflame again and rekindle the warm satisfaction of walking with our Creator.

Resources

Anne Bèrubè, *The Burnout Antidote: A Spiritual Guide to Empowerment for Empaths, Over-givers, and Highly Sensitive People* (Woodbury, MN: Llewellyn, 2022).

Josh Roberie, *Surviving Religious Burnout: Get Out of Your Spiritual Rut and Start Enjoying a Meaningful Christianity* (self-published, 2020).

CHAPTER ELEVEN

A Time to Converse with Jesus: Learning Immanuel Interactive Two-Way Journaling

Denice C. MacKenzie RN, CS

Denice C. Mackenzie became a disciple in Boulder, CO in 1978 and has lived in Boston, New Jersey, Denver, and Boulder. She currently lives in Northglenn, Colorado with her husband, Bob. Denice works in full-time private practice as a board-certified Christian psychotherapist and psychiatric nurse clinical specialist, where she often uses interactive prayer and journaling tools. She and Bob started a prayer ministry in their church in 2010 and have enjoyed teaching classes and practicing interactive prayer in their family group, online groups, and with their podcast and website. Denice especially enjoys long walks with her husband, her cats, bookstores and writing, poetry, podcasting, cooking, hiking, and animals of all kinds.

Do you ever struggle to find the peace and rest spoken of in Matthew 11:28–29 but find it elusive? Do you sometimes tire of doing things *for* God instead of *with* him? Above all else that we do, God created us for deep attachment and connection with him. God wants you to experience him with all parts of your being, with your heart, soul, mind, and strength, not just intellectually. Your soul and spirit will wither without that connection. Adam was not simply created to till the garden or to name the animals. He was created to connect with God, so together they would explore creation and enjoy one another. Jesus longs for interactive connection with you in the same way. Attachment is meant to be two-way and conversational with God, so he gave you his Spirit to ensure that you could access his heart and his thoughts. You can do this with any member of the trinity that you feel most comfortable with, but for purposes of simplicity, we will refer to Jesus throughout this chapter.

These exercises are meant to lead you into deeper attachment with God. There is an entire science now dedicated to the study of human attachment with God and others. When done as close to daily as possible, even for just five minutes, these exercises build your attachment "muscles" and create new wiring. For that reason, it can feel awkward and difficult at first. As with any new skill, as you practice more, it becomes more a part of you. These exercises are based on attachment science and designed to engage both sides of our brains, the left logical and the right relational, which then filter down to all aspects of our being. We are created to enjoy all the benefits of connecting with God interactively, such as increased joy, increased relational capacity with others, and greater love. This helps with our human connections as well, since both use the same attachment pathways.

Adam did his works out of a deep abiding with God. He walked with God in the cool of the garden. I envision God teaching and enjoying him during those walks. If we put even godly works before relationship with God himself, we can feel dry and depleted, longing for reprieve. Just like a branch cannot get nourishment from the vine unless it stays very closely attached, we too need reminders for deeper abiding. As you do these simple two-way interactive prayers, please give yourself permission to playfully explore conversations with Jesus that you may not be familiar with. They provide a starting point from which you can launch into the deep.

As I grew in my capacity to interact with the Holy Spirit, I found that it was like talking with my best friend, rather than presenting a list of needs to God. It became much more fun to do things with God, rather than for God. It brought so much joy to me personally that I cannot picture going back to the way I used to pray, which was mostly one-way and composed of lists, requests, and expressing my heart, but without waiting to "hear his reply" to my soul. I did almost all the talking, hardly catching a breath in my prayers because, I reasoned, the Bible was where he would do his talking to me. If I had done that with my friends, they would most likely not be eager to converse with me. Thankfully, we have a very patient God.

Now I mostly listen. I have learned that he is always ready to answer me and always hears my thoughts before I ask. I've learned that both prayer and reading his word are meant to be two-way and interactive, within the guidelines of the Bible, centered on Jesus, and led by his Holy Spirit. It is very freeing to know that if I'm willing to listen, I can know the heart and mind of God on any issue in my life and experience his heart for me, not just intellectually but relationally and emotionally. Jesus longs for this with each one of us. Rest in the love that Jesus has for you. Just as he went away both to hear from and talk with the Father, he waits for you. As you build on the prayer foundation you've already established, learning deeper ways of abiding, may you be abundantly blessed and refreshed.

"Come to me, all who labor and are heavy laden, and I will give you rest. Take my yoke upon you, and learn from me, for I am gentle and lowly in heart, and you will find rest for your souls." (Matthew 11:28–29 ESV)

"Abide in me, and I in you. As the branch cannot bear fruit by itself, unless it abides in the vine, neither can you, unless you abide in me." (John 15:4 ESV)

For who among men knows the thoughts of a man except the spirit of the man which is in him? Even so the thoughts of God no one knows except the Spirit of God. Now we have received, not the spirit of the world, but the Spirit who is from God, so that we may know the things freely given to us by God. (1 Corinthians 2:11–12 NASB1995)

"I am the good shepherd; I know my sheep and my sheep know me... The sheep listen to his voice. He calls his own sheep by name and leads them out." (John 10:14, 2–3)

It is the Spirit who testifies, because the Spirit is the truth. (1 John 5:6)

"I have many more things to say to you, but you cannot bear them now. But when He, the Spirit of truth, comes, He will guide you into all the truth; for He will not speak on His own initiative, but whatever He hears, He will speak; and He will disclose to you what is to come. He will glorify Me, for He will take of Mine and will disclose it to you." (John 16:12–14 NASB1995)

What an amazing God we have! He wants to know us and for us to truly know him. Since the word "know" often refers to experiential "knowing" rather than intellectual in the Bible (see Glenn Giles' essay on *yada'*), we can know from attachment science[57] that this goes beyond intellectual knowing. We have read that the lies we've believed about God, ourselves, and others have led us into sin, which leads to death (Romans 8:5–12), so it's imperative to truly know God and listen to his heart. He gave us his Holy Spirit to direct and guide us into all truth and life.

Take a moment to slowly read the last verse posted above, John 16:12–14, so this will be more meaningful for you. Jesus is the way, the truth, and the life (John 14:6), and he is in relationship with us, guiding us into all truth through his word and his Spirit. When we are guided into truth within a relationship, our brains learn it better than just reading about something that is true. Think about all you learned as a young child. It came out of a relational context. In fact, children spend all of their first three years in their right, relational brains. Perhaps this is why we need to become as little children to enter the kingdom of God. Research shows children and adults both learn better within a securely attached relationship.[58]

In addition to God's word as truth, the Bible states that Jesus is the truth, and his Spirit is the truth (John 14:6; 1 John 5:6; John 16:12–14), so you have a relationship with truth. The Holy Spirit will guide you into all truth as you explore the Scriptures and focus on Jesus in these exercises. Just as God taught Adam as they walked in the garden together, it's good to know you are never alone in this process. We will review some guidelines and checks below.

---

57. https://mbird.com/psychology/attachment-theory-and-your-relationship-with-god/

58. Dr. Sue Johnson and Kenny Sanderfer, *Created for Connection: The "Hold Me Tight" Guide for Christian Couples* (New York: Little Brown Spark, 2016).

When we refer to the concept of interacting with God about something in a two-way manner, we are referring to this process of slowing down and attuning to the Holy Spirit to let him guide us into all truth. God is very relational and enjoys being with you, sharing his thoughts with you and hearing your thoughts about your present concerns (1 Corinthians 2:11–12). He accepts and loves you right where you are. Many of you may already have your own way of doing this, which works well for you. That is great! Use these disciplines to strengthen those pathways. If you have had a hard time experiencing God in the past, this is one way that can simplify the process, and help you to pass it along to others as well.

God created the right brain to be almost fully relational and experiential, while the left brain is more logical and analytical. We need to engage both sides of our brain to fully understand and experience something. Just as you cannot fully "know" what it is like to ride a bike by only reading an instruction manual (left brain), we too need to "get on the bike" and allow ourselves to fully experience the balance that is meant to occur between our left and right brains as we engage God relationally.

Schooling, lectures, and books have trained us to learn from mostly the left side of our brains, and that is why this can feel a bit unnatural and even frightening at first. "Will we be led astray? Will we lose our foundational footing? Where are the brakes?" Using the "Conversing with Jesus" exercises below you are training more of your right brain, the part made for relational attachment and experience. There is nothing you need to understand first or "get right" to do these exercises, except what has been briefly explained so far. Since the exercise is mostly experiential, you won't be able to understand it by only reading about it, you must experience it. Simply hop on the bike and begin your ride! He wants to experience your heart, and have you experience his. If it feels a bit wobbly at first just let him know, and most importantly, keep practicing. Soon you will be enjoying a new-felt freedom as you learn to ride tandem with God.

As in any relationship, good listening skills require that we quiet our minds and open our hearts to what the person is really saying, giving up our assumptions. We must ask ourselves "Are we willing to be changed in this conversation?" It takes great love, attunement, and courage to see the world through someone else's eyes. It is no different in our relationship with Jesus. To surrender our own agenda and expectations of who we think he is and who we are in relationship to him, as well as what we think he is going to say to us, is always the first and most essential step.

Consider the following:

Surrender – Borrowing from *Merriam-Webster,* this can mean to "cease resistance and submit to someone's authority, or to give something over to someone more powerful." Unfortunately, this definition as applied to God can raise white flags with some of us, literally! When referring to God, we need to see ourselves instead as aligning with God's will for us, joining his invitation to partner with him and see the world through his perspective, or have "God-sight." Our perspective is still important to him, however. When we fully surrender to him because we want to see the world through his eyes, he meets us in love where we are at. He then gently shows us his good and sovereign will for our lives, which is always better than anything we could imagine on our own.

Attunement – Being able to get outside ourselves enough to experience another's presence, whereby we are able to hear them and understand them, without judgment. Our awareness of who they are deepens as we put ourselves in their shoes. This goes beyond empathy to create an interactive experience that is in harmony with theirs.

As you approach these exercises, which may be a little different for some of you, realize that God honors your heart and intention. This is not meant to replace the Bible. You are not asking for new revelation; you are simply getting further clarity and direction about what the Bible already says, or about your life in general. We are learning to interact with the living Jesus within biblical parameters with the help of the Holy Spirit. All three should be in agreement, always. The Scriptures teach that we can know the mind and heart of God, and we can synchronize our minds with his so that we may know the things he chooses to reveal to us (1 Corinthians 2:10–16).

Don't worry about whether your impressions are from God or yourself at first. They are probably a little of both because you are simply synchronizing your mind with his, as you would do in any conversation. After you are finished with the exercise, it is wise to check it against the "Filter Checks" (see below). The purpose of this is to ensure that what we sense from the Holy Spirit is always in line with Scripture, since the written word of God is the only fully reliable and final source for knowing God's character and will.

One of the functions of the Holy Spirit is to reveal God's heart to us, which will always be in line with scriptural principles and concepts, even if the Spirit doesn't exactly quote a particular verse to us. He may reveal God's heart for us in other ways that could include memories, pictures, songs, emotions, or just a "felt sense." *We can never elevate our "experience" of God above the written and inspired truths of God's word.* That is why we want to check how we sense that God is guiding us against the filter checks, and then check with one or two other Christians as well. Our brains learn better in community, and this helps us stay out of error.

Important Note: Do the "Filter Checks" *after* you have finished your exercise. If you do them *during* the exercise, your left, analytical brain can quickly shut your right, relational brain down. So just write without filtering your thoughts, then filter check later.

Before Each Exercise:

Quiet and Surrender

Psalm 46:10 states, "Cease striving and know that I am God" (NASB1995). This implies interactive understanding. Before we can interact with God's Spirit, we must cease striving and prepare to hear his heart for us.

Quiet your mind by breathing in two or three deep breaths. Slowly exhale. Count to four on both the in breath and out breath and hold for four seconds each. Then simply quiet for at least two minutes, not expecting anything. This is to help you slow down your mind to the speed of your heart, so you approach him with all parts of your being. Do the quieting throughout your journaling whenever you get stuck. It is an essential first step that cannot be skipped, especially in our fast-paced, intellectually driven world. If your mind wanders, just notice that and bring it back to focusing on your breath, not on your thoughts.

Surrender your expectations of what you think you will receive as you listen to him through your spirit, to his Spirit. Say a quick surrender prayer, and ask for his guidance and protection, trusting that you will receive it. Remember that he honors your intention to hear him more deeply. Don't fear the enemy's distractions—most of the time, God will eliminate that for you. Simply be still, keep your eyes on Jesus, and see the victory that he will bring you today.

Exercise Basics

Gratitude

This part is significant and is included in each exercise. Don't skip over this, as it primes your brain for relational connection, based on the latest research. Try to include something you feel genuinely grateful for that makes you feel warm and settled inside, not just something you know you are "supposed" to be thankful for without an emotional connection.

Interaction

Interact with God as you would in any conversation. If you were to tell a friend something on your heart, and they said nothing in return, you would think that a little odd. In the same way, God has a reply to your gratitude and to any thought you may have in the journaling process, or during your day. He is always conversing with us through his Spirit, so it's a matter of training our ears to hear what his Spirit is saying. You can ask questions for clarity, bring up topics on your heart, or just listen to what is on God's heart more fully. There are many ways to interact with a loved one, and the same is true with Jesus. This is one way that you may find helpful.

Whatever feels most comfortable to you, as long as it is from your heart, he values. He simply enjoys being with you. You can think of your interaction as journaling, texting, writing a letter, making a phone call, or showing up in person. His response to you can also be varied. The Bible states that he communicated with the prophets, the apostles, and everyday people through dreams, symbols, miracles, objects, memories, words, visions, feelings, bodily sensations, and concepts. Sometimes he would even communicate through animals or the weather. This is why we need to be able to engage with him with all parts of our being, and not only expect him to respond to us with the left, logical side of our brain.

Keep a Journal

It's important to write down what you receive from God so you can check the filter checks, refer to these conversations later, revisit them, share them with others, and add to them.

Listening to Immanuel – Two-Way Immanuel Journaling / Conversing with Jesus

The following simple steps are taken from *Joyful Journey*.[59] Each of the five main steps (Steps 2–6), or statements, aligns with one of the five levels of the brain, so when finished you feel fully "heard" and understood by God. Using a personal journal or recording can lead to rich insights over time as you revisit your connection times with God. Journaling takes more time, but the rewards are worth it! With your journal in hand (or phone, recorder, etc.), after quieting and a prayer of surrender, you are ready to embark on your journey. Remember, you were made for this!

---

59. Used with permission by Jim Wilder, with certain additions by this author. See www. LifeModelWorks.org.

STEP ONE – "**Gratitude.**" Write down anything you genuinely appreciate to God. Include some details, if possible, including your senses and emotions. This helps activate the right, relational attachment center in your brain.

Dear God, I'm thankful for... (Example): *"The fresh smell of grass this morning after it rained, and how I was able to sense your presence as I read your word today out on the lawn."*

Dear child of mine... This is God's response to your gratitude. Write what comes to mind without filtering or wondering whether it's from God or not. You can check the filter checks later. (Example): *"I am glad that you love the smell of grass."* (Or you just may sense God's shared pleasure with you as you smell the grass together, or a picture in your mind's eye, of walking hand in hand with him as you stroll through the grass.) And *"I am with you as you read my word, guiding your heart and mind."*

Issue (optional): At this point you can lift an issue to God that you are concerned about, or proceed without an issue, to see wherever Jesus wants to take you. Think of what you get here as his attunement to you, which produces a strengthened relational pathway with him. As you become more centered, aware of God's presence, you may or may not find the "answer" to your issue. Remember to surrender that in your opening prayer and accept whatever he may have for you first. Over time, I have found this relational attunement is key to my ability to understand any issue in my life from God's perspective. I need to know he understands me first, and is in my corner; otherwise, I may misinterpret even Scripture harshly, as applied toward myself or others. He is attuning to your heart, and you are attuning to his heart about you, not the issue. You are much more important to him than the issue at hand. With that understanding, you can then go back to this attached place of connection and explore the issue further, but the relational attachment always comes first. If you lift an issue to him, the rest of the exercise usually is in response to your issue, how he sees you in it, and his attunement to you about it. If you do not, this exercise can address anything; just wait and see what surfaces and comes to your mind.

STEP TWO – "**I see you.**" Write this statement in your journal, and pause. This is what God is saying to you. Scripturally, God saw, heard, empathized with, and responded to the Israelites in Egypt when they were crying out to him; and he sent them Moses. There are many other biblical references to this process. He is saying, "_____ (your name), or my dear child, I see you." Next, quiet, close your eyes if you need to, and just notice what God may see in you. Write from God's perspective what he sees in you right now, what you sense he puts on your heart, including spiritual, emotional, or physical observations. (Example: *I see you at your desk; you are feeling overwhelmed,*" or "*Your shoulders are tight,*" or "*I see your longing to do things well.*") Write the first thing that comes to your mind without filtering or wondering whether it is from God or not. You will use the filter checks at the very end. Simply trust that his Spirit of truth is guiding you, for now.

STEP THREE – "**I hear you.**" Write this sentence in your journal as if from God's perspective. Pause, close your eyes, and quiet, again surrendering your agenda. Just notice what comes to mind without filtering. In any of these steps you can form it as a question rather than a statement, such as, "God, what do you hear me saying to myself, you, or others?" (Example: *I hear you wondering how you'll be able to hear me, or how you'll ever get it all done,*" or "*I heard your prayer, or what you said to your spouse, child, or friend last night.*") Repeat the instructions in Step Two, but instead of using "I see you," you are using "I hear you" in this step.

STEP FOUR – "**I understand how big this is for you and how you cannot handle it on your own.**" (Example: *I want you to know that I am here for you in all you undertake, to bear your burdens and hold you up. I understand how this situation feels all-consuming to you.*) Repeat the instructions in Steps Two and Three, using this starter sentence, or pose it as a question.

STEP FIVE – **"I am glad to be with you and treat your weakness tenderly."** How does God express his desire to participate in your life and to let you know you are not alone? (Example: *"I delight in your desire to_____," or "I enjoyed being with you today when you were resting; I am with you in weakness and strength," or "I see your discouragement when you are sad and feel rejected. I will never leave you.")* Repeat the same steps as above.

STEP SIX – **"I am doing something about what you are going through."** How is God directing you in this time? (Example: *"Remember the friend who called to encourage you last week? I put you upon their heart," or "Come away and rest with me. I offer you times of refreshing, new energy, and vision. I will strengthen you.")* End with gratitude for what God has shown you.

STEP SEVEN – **Read what you have written aloud,** preferably to someone else. Check it against the filter checks (see below).

Summary: The Main Principles of Two-Way Journaling:

1. Remember first and foremost, you are made for this kind of connection with God, just as Adam and Eve were. It is the most natural state of being with God.

2. Surrender your agenda and pray at the beginning of each journaling time, for protection from the enemy, guidance from Jesus, and attunement with the Holy Spirit of truth. Trust that God honors your intention to seek him and to know the truth, just as you would honor a child who wanted to speak with you face to face.

3. Always quiet for at least two minutes, if possible, and start with two-way interactive gratitude. This primes the brain for relational connection. "Enter his gates with thanksgiving and his courts with praise; give thanks to him and praise his name" (Psalm 100:4).

4. Keep your focus on Jesus. Let him lead you relationally.

You can ask him for guidance for the next step in the process. This is not a left-brain process. You don't have to figure it out before, during, or after your interaction or do it exactly right. It is a relational interaction, and there is much room for grace, forgiveness, and learning relational skills.

5. If you get stuck and don't know what to do, or lose your connection, go back to your appreciation at the beginning, and ask him about the problem from that place of attachment.

6. Review the "Filter Checks."

7. Share your journaling with others.

Filter Checks: How Do I Know It's Really God?

Use these only after you are finished with your journaling, never during the process. If you feel at peace about what you've written, check it against the filter checks. If it passes most or all of them, read it aloud to one or two other safe people, just as you received it, without interpretation.

1. Is it consistent with God's word—not only actual verses but the underlying principles of the Word and of God's character (2 Timothy 3:16)?

2. Does it bring life and heal? God's word is more life giving than our words (John 10:10).

3. Do we experience his thoughts higher than our thoughts? Does it bring different and better insight and quality, deeper clarity, understanding, and revelation (Isaiah 55:8)?

4. Does it pass the *peace/shalom* test of Colossians 3:15? Do you feel greater peace?

5. Does it bear other fruit, now and when carried out (Galatians 5:22)?

a. Immediate: resolution, peace, love, excitement, awe, clarity

b. Long term: attitudes and expectations that are more God-centered

6. God's confrontations are gentle and caring (Matthew 11:29–30; Romans 8:1). Jesus' admonitions to those who want to follow him are gentle. Harsh condemnations are from our own background or from the accuser.

7. Check with your community (assuming it is healthy) for confirmation.

   a. Do other Christians recognize it as coming from God and in line with God's word and character? Check it out with two or three trusted Christian advisors before you act on something you've heard that impacts your life or your relationships in any significant way, such as moving to another location, changing jobs, or leaving a relationship (Proverbs 27:17; Matthew 18:19; Colossians 3:15).

   b. If another Christian senses it's not from God, ask them why. Pray for discernment, as this could be an area of growth for both parties.

8. Does it draw us nearer to God and glorify him (Hebrews 10:22; James 4:8; 1 Corinthians 10:31)?

9. Is it supported by circumstances and reality? Does it come true over time (Ephesians 5:15; Romans 8:28)?

10. Does it ring true in your heart when you interact with God and the Holy Spirit in prayer (Romans 8:1, 26; John 14:26)?

11. Does it line up with your past experience of hearing God? As you become more familiar with God's heart through your own experience and through the ways his heart is revealed in Scripture, you recognize it better (1 John 2:5, 21).

Getting Unstuck

Everyone runs into blockages at some point along the way. Some blockages require an Immanuel Prayer session with two trained facilitators (see resources), or counseling. Most of them, however, can be resolved fairly easily, although not always quickly. Remember, this is what you are made for, so the enemy is throwing up the blockage. Even though you are made for it, some of us didn't get foundational relational pathways reinforced very much in childhood. The good news is that the brain is always relationally resilient and can learn and grow regardless of our age. These pathways can be created with Jesus in this exercise. It will just take longer for some than others. No matter what, please don't panic or give up. The following steps will heal most blockages.

Go back to the breathing step and spend more time there until your mind is quiet. If you cannot calm your mind, try going on a walk and talking with Jesus, or listening to instrumental music.

Surrender your expectations of timing, content, outcome, or anything upsetting to Jesus. Pray this daily: *"God, I put all of me into your hands, all parts of my heart, soul, mind, and strength. Take away my fears and help me trust you. You have full access to all of me and all my expectations for this exercise. Please give me full access to all your love for me, God, and remove any blockages I may have to connecting with you. Bind the enemy under your feet and authority, Jesus; I only want to hear from your Holy Spirit."*

Spend more time quieting throughout your day, several times per day. Notice how it helps you be more present, effective, and attuned. Set an alarm to remind you if needed. The minimum amount of breathing and quieting most of us need is two minutes before our "mind chatter" begins to quiet down. You may need more, however. The biggest hindrance we hear is, "I just can't get my mind to stop thinking." Practicing quieting several times a day will help you to prepare the way for intimate interactive listening times with Jesus.

Just ask Jesus: "Just ask Jesus" should become your default phrase for everything! A simple prayer after quieting, surrender, and gratitude can go something like: *"Jesus, I know you are omnipresent. Since I cannot sense your presence right now, please show me what is blocking my perception of your interactive presence,"* then listen without filters, write it down, and check it against the filter checks. If that does not resolve it, don't hesitate to reach out for help.[60]

Appreciation: Spending more time in two-way appreciation with God will grow your relational pathways and bring greater joy. You may have to stay in this phase for a while before you take the dive into deeper waters with Steps 2–6. One woman who couldn't hear or sense Jesus' presence at all in the beginning spent two full years in this phase before she could interact with Jesus back and forth. Today, she teaches classes on interactive two-way journaling. For most people, it will not take this long, but remember it is worth it, no matter what it takes, because not only will it help your relationship with God, but with others as well.

Spend more time interacting with God in Scripture: As you are reading your Bible or beforehand, ask God if there is anything he wants to lead you to, or to highlight for you, within the scripture you've chosen. If he brings your attention to a certain verse, phrase, or connecting scripture, spend as much time as you need there. Ask clarifying questions as needed, and listen for his response. Write them down. Over time, you will gain confidence in this back-and-forth process as you sense his "still small voice" within you leading you through his word. This will enliven your knowledge of the Scriptures and help you to trust this interaction in other areas of your life.

Check all these things against the filter checks and share them with a few close friends.

---

60. Taken from "The Immanuel Approach," Dr. Karl C. Lehman.

Suggestions for Incorporating Immanuel Conversations into Your Lifestyle

(See resources below for how to put these steps into practice)

1. Cultivate two-way gratitude in your daily life, surrendering and quieting as close to daily as possible.

2. Practice two-way interaction in your times with God when reading the Bible or in prayer, in addition to two-way journaling. Make it your lifestyle.

3. Keep a journal, labeling your interactions with brief titles. Reread periodically to see the themes that God has been bringing to you over a particular time in your life. Begin from what you have written the previous day, for the next day's journaling, or start with a new topic, question, praise, or verse. The possibilities are endless.

4. Form your own small group: Share your interactions with others by forming a triad. Always be open to input about your journaling, be humble, and never impose on others what you sense from God.

5. Join a Forming class when offered (see resources).

6. Join other interactive journaling and prayer groups offered online through the Life Model (see resources).

7. Receive a prayer ministry session. This is a focused time with two trained prayer ministers using Immanuel Prayer. This is especially helpful if you are stuck in an issue or feel a wall in your ability to connect with God or others (check www.AlignwithGod.org, www.alivewell.org, or www.facetofaceministries.org). All these ministries use Life Model research and principles.

8. In fellowship, when someone is hurting or needs prayer, invite them to quiet and listen to what Jesus may have for them. Guide them to tell you what the Spirit is putting on their hearts. Amazing insights have been gained by this simple step!

Thank you for your courage to embark on this journey using these interactive journaling tools. As you go forward keeping in step with his Spirit, focused on Jesus, and based on his word, may you experience all the blessings and peace that God has for you with all parts of your being. Let this become your lifestyle through practicing these disciplines, and notice your joy being "made full," as you grow into the relational being God has created you to be. Most importantly, remember, you are made for this!

But now I come to You; and these things I speak in the world so that they may have My joy made full in themselves... I have made Your name known to them, and will make it known, so that the love with which You loved Me may be in them, and I in them. (John 17:13, 26 NASB1995)

Resources

The Life Model and Jim Wilder, www.lifemodel.org.

J. Wilder, A. Kang, J. Loppnow, and S. Loppnow, *Joyful Journey* – instructions for journaling and setting up small groups to practice (Los Angeles, CA: Presence and Practice, 2020).

J. Wilder, J. Friesen, A. Berlin, R. Kopeck, M. Poole, *Living from the Heart Jesus Gave You* (East Peoria, IL: Shepherd's House, 2016).

Align with God Ministries and podcast at www.alignwithGod.org. The podcast breaks down the Immanuel journaling steps into smaller units and leads you through an exercise.

Alive and Well Prayer Ministries, offering Immanuel Prayer sessions and training at www.aliveandwell.org

Face to Face ministries and podcast, offering Immanuel Prayer sessions and training at www.facetofaceministries.org

Dr. Karl C. Lehman, *The Immanuel Approach,* at www.immanuelapproach.com. Dr. Lehman is the codeveloper of the Immanuel Prayer approach and uses it in his practice.

Peter Scazzero, "Emotionally Healthy Spirituality" podcast and books.

David Takle, *Forming,* www.forming-course.com.

Byron Parson, www.byronparson.com for Forming groups, books, and resources.

CHAPTER TWELVE

Yada':
The Unique Heart of True Christianity
Dr. Glenn Giles, MDiv

Dr. Glenn Giles is Founder, Director, and Professor of Bible and Theology at Rocky Mountain School of Ministry and Theology in Denver, Colorado. He received his Master of Divinity from Lincoln Christian University and his Master of Theology from Trinity Evangelical Divinity School, and after doing doctoral work at Marquette University in religious studies, he completed his PhD in biblical studies at Trinity Theological Seminary in 2013. He has been adjunct professor of Bible at Lincoln Christian University since 2008. Glenn is an elder in the Denver Church of Christ and has written and taught extensively on the idea of *yada'* and the bidirectional experiential relationship God desires between him and his people and people with one another. Glenn has been married to his beautiful wife, Linda, for forty-nine years and has three children and five grandchildren.

For many years I have been contemplating the specialness of our ICOC fellowship in the area of the heart. When I came to our fellowship, I found the very special relational aspect of true Christianity. I have called it the "heart" ever since I was studied with in Milwaukee. What I experienced was different from what I had experienced in any religious group before. It was the difference between being a person who knew about God and had some association with him and being a person who truly knows God through a true personal relationship with him. The things our churches have gone through during the last twenty years have caused me to search the Scriptures to better understand that which I have been calling "heart." In the last few months, I have come to understand that the heart is what is involved in the Old Testament concept of *yada',* the Hebrew word for "know."

In this essay, I will attempt to explain that concept, a concept that I think distinguishes us from nearly all other movements of today that I am aware of,[61] a concept that I would urge everyone to hold onto and never surrender, a concept that when experienced is the watershed of spiritual life and death.

> *"Not everyone who says to me, 'Lord, Lord,' will enter the kingdom of heaven, but only he who does the will of my Father who is in heaven. Many will say to me on that day, 'Lord, Lord, did we not prophesy in your name, and in your name drive out demons and perform many miracles?' Then I will tell them plainly, 'I never **knew** you. Away from me, you evildoers'"* (Matthew 7:21–23, emphasis mine).

For a long time, I have felt that this was talking about a personal relationship with God but did not understand the depth of what it meant until I studied out the Hebrew word *yada'.*[62] The big question is "What does it mean to be known by God and to know God?"

The Greek word here in Matthew 7:23 is *ginosko.* Of the 946 times *yada'* is found in the Hebrew OT, over 490 times it is translated *ginosko* in the LXX (the Greek translation of the Hebrew Old Testament). Hence *ginosko* is the major Greek word used for *yada'.* The Greeks, however, did not have a word that translates *yada'* with its full meaning. The closest term the Greeks had was *ginosko.* The Greek term *ginosko* designates predominately an intellectual concept, which is not the predominate concept involved in *yada'.*[63] The major emphasis of *yada'* includes subjective dimensions of knowing, not just the objective.

> In Greek philosophy *ginoskein* has a predominant meaning of "intellectual looking at" an object of scrutiny and strongly connotes objectivity... For the Hebrews *yada'* is more by the heart than by the mind, and the knowing arises

---

61. That does not mean there are not those out there who have experienced what we (or I) have but that generally I am unaware of them in my experience.

62. The information on Hebrew word occurrences in this essay are from John R. Kohlenberger III and James Swanson, *The Hebrew-English Concordance to the Old Testament with the New International Version* (Grand Rapids: Zondervan, 1998), hereafter designated as HECOT. Page 617.

63. *Theological Dictionary of the Old Testament,* G. Johannes Botterweck and Helmer Ringgren, eds, translated by J. T. Willis (Grand Rapids: Eerdmans, 1997), vol. 5, 453, hereafter designated by TDOT. Cf., Edwin Hatch and Henry Redpath, A Concordance to the Septuagint, 3 vols. (Grand Rapids: Baker, 1983), vol 1, 267–70.

not by standing back from in order to look at, but by active and intentional engagement in lived experience... The Hebrews had no word that corresponds exactly to our words "mind" or "intellect."[64]

"*Yada'*" has the basic meaning of "to perceive, know."[65] Its semantic range is broad and also embraces definitions such as "find out," "know by experience," "recognize," "acknowledge," "know a person, be acquainted with," "be skillful," "teach," and "make known,"[66] as well as "to notice," "learn," "to know sexually, have intercourse with, copulate," "to have experience," and "to take care of someone."[67] This word for the most part involves knowledge gained through experience.[68] It thus indicates experiential knowledge.[69] This is contrary to much of our modern-day understanding of "knowledge" and its acquisition, which largely involves pure thought by one's own contemplation or mere verbal transmission of information from teacher to student in a classroom setting. That is not to say that *yada'* does not include these types of knowledge and teaching but that it has as its major dimension experientially gained or relationally gained knowledge.

With respect to "knowing" God, the Old Testament use of this term is enlightening. Consider the following verses:

---

64. *Theological Lexicon of the Old Testament*, translated by Mark E. Biddle (Peabody, MA: Hendrickson Publishers, Inc., 1997), vol. 2, 514, hereafter designated as TLOT, concurs, stating:... the meaning of yada' in Hebr. would be insufficiently stated if one were to limit it strictly to the cognitive aspect... without simultaneously taking into account the contractual aspect of the meaning, e.g., the fact that yada' does not merely indicate a theoretical relation, a pure act of thought, but that knowledge, as yada' intends it, is realized through practical involvement with the obj. of knowledge. *The New International Dictionary of Old Testament Theology and Exegesis*, 5 vols., edited by Willem A. VanGemeren (Grand Rapids: Zondervan, 1997), vol. 2, 410 (hereafter designated as NIDOTT) also concurs, stating, "The fundamentally relational character of knowing (over against a narrow intellectual sense) can be discerned, not the least in that both God and human beings can be subject and object of the vb."

65. Ernst Jenni and Claus Westermann, *TLOT* vol. 2, 508.

66. Francis Brown, S. R. Driver, and C. A. Briggs in *A Hebrew and English Lexicon of the Old Testament* (Oxford: Clarendon, 1976), 393–94, hereafter noted as BDB.

67. TLOT, vol. 2, 390–92.

68. Lawrence O. Richards, *Christian Education: Seeking to Become Like Jesus Christ* (Grand Rapids: Zondervan, 1975), 33.

69. There are only a relatively few times that it means "intellectual" knowledge.

"Therefore I will teach (yada') them—
    this time I will teach (yada') them
    my power and might.
Then they will know (yada')
    that my name is the LORD." (Jeremiah 16:21)

Knowing God comes from him causing them to experience his power and might.

"Then they will know (yada') that I am the LORD,
    when I set fire to Egypt
    and all her helpers are crushed." (Ezekiel 30:8)

Knowledge of God comes through experiencing his character of justice and wrath. This concept of to "know that I am the Lord" occurs over sixty-five times in Ezekiel alone, indicating relational knowledge coming through experiencing his judgments.

"I will betroth you to Me forever;
Yes, I will betroth you to Me in righteousness and in justice,
in loving kindness and in compassion,
And I will betroth you to Me in faithfulness.
Then you will know (yada') the LORD." (Hosea 2:19–20 NASB)

Knowing the Lord is a result of experiencing his righteousness, justice, loving kindness, compassion, and faithfulness.

"He will revive us after two days;
He will raise us up on the third day,
That we may live before Him.
"So let us know (yada'), let us press on to know (yada') the LORD.
His going forth is as certain as the dawn;
And He will come to us like the rain,
Like the spring rain watering the earth." (Hosea 6:2–3 NASB1995)

Knowledge of God is obtained through experiencing him reviving them and giving them rain. They would not know God, however, if they did not press on in faithfulness to experience his character. Knowing God comes from experiencing God's faithfulness, mercy, and provision.

One of the most important passages in the Old Testament is Jeremiah 31:34:

> *"No longer will a man teach his neighbor,*
> *or a man his brother, saying, 'Know (yada') the LORD,'*
> *because they will all know (yada') me,*
> *from the least of them to the greatest,*
> *declares the LORD.*
> *"For I will forgive their wickedness*
> *and will remember their sins no more."*

The word "for" here indicates that knowing the Lord comes as a result of a person experiencing the Lord's forgiveness and his forgetting their sins. Knowing God thus comes by experiencing his grace.[70]

All of these passages indicate that knowing God involves interpersonal experience with his character. God is allowing people to know him through experiencing his character. Knowing God, however, also involves our response to him. It is associated with one's obedience to him (1 Samuel 2:12; Job 18:21), fear of him (1 Kings 8:43; 2 Chronicles 6:33), serving him (1 Chronicles 28:9), belief in him (Isaiah 43:10), trust in him (Psalm 9:10; Proverbs 3:5–6), confession of one's sin (Psalm 32:5), and knowledge of the Torah, or his word (Psalm 119:79).[71] It thus "involves not just theoretical knowledge but acceptance of the divine will for one's own life."[72]

Knowing God can be summarized as coming from one's personal life experience of the relational blessings or discipline of God as a result of one's trusting in and following him. Knowing God involves experiencing his character and willingly submitting to him as Lord.

So, we see that when used in the New Testament, in a Hebrew context (Matthew was written to a Jewish audience), the word

---

70. To know God, as Terence E. Fretheim states, "is to be in a right relationship with him, with characteristics of love, trust, respect, and open communication," NIDOTTE, vol.2, 413.

71. TLOT, vol. 2. 518.

72. TDOT, vol. 5, 478.

"know" (*ginosko* in Greek) takes on more than an intellectual concept. It takes on an experiential interpersonal relational meaning. Therefore, when we see the statement in Matthew 7:23, "I never knew you," it is not talking about intellectual knowledge but character or relational knowledge. This fits perfectly into the context of Matthew 7:15–23, which states:

> *"Watch out for false prophets. They come to you in sheep's clothing, but inwardly they are ferocious wolves. By their fruit you will recognize (epiginosko, an intensive form of ginosko)[73] them. Do people pick grapes from thorn bushes, or figs from thistles? Likewise, every good tree bears good fruit, but a bad tree bears bad fruit. A good tree cannot bear bad fruit, and a bad tree cannot bear good fruit. Every tree that does not bear good fruit is cut down and thrown into the fire. Thus, by their fruit you will recognize (epiginosko) them.*
>
> *"Not everyone who says to me, 'Lord, Lord,' will enter the kingdom of heaven, but only he who does the will of my Father who is in heaven. Many will say to me on that day, 'Lord, Lord, did we not prophesy in your name, and in your name drive out demons and perform many miracles?' Then I will tell them plainly, 'I never knew (ginosko) you. Away from me, you evildoers!'"*

Our knowledge, our *yada*, of people occurs when we experience their character (verses 15–20). You can be sure that people are false prophets if they do not produce good fruit. God's knowing of us also occurs by his experiencing our character (verses 21–23). Even though one might do things, things that are good, there can be lacking an interpersonal relationship, a heart knowing. As is typical in Matthew, relationship with God was more than outward show or actions; it must involve the heart (e.g., Matthew 15:8–9).

God tests us to see what is in our heart to "know" us. Consider Deuteronomy 8:1–2:

> *Be careful to follow every command I am giving you today, so that you may live and increase and may enter and possess the land that the LORD promised on oath to your forefathers. Remember how the LORD your God led you all the way in the desert these forty years, to humble you and to test you in order to know (yada') what was in your heart, whether or not you would keep his commands.*

---

73. This word is also, the majority of the time, the Greek translation of yada' in the LXX.

Note the use of the word "know" here. Surely an all-knowing God "knew" what was in their hearts from an intellectual perspective. So, what does this mean? Our study of *yada'* would indicate that God wanted to experience what was in their hearts through experiencing their obedience. This is how God knows them and can know us! It is not just about raw works but about relationship experienced through actions toward God and he toward us. He wants to know us personally and wants us to know him personally. He wants to experience our character. He wants to live out life with us, it seems. Just as his love for us would not be real unless his heart and actions worked together to allow us to experience his character, so our love for him is not real unless our heart and actions work together to allow him to experience us. No wonder James 2 states that faith without works is dead and that works complete our faith! Works complete our personal relationship with God. They do not make us merit that relationship (that is a totally erroneous perspective). Obedience is our allowing God to experience us. This is how God knows us.

When I reflect on what I experienced in our movement, it brings me great joy to see how those who studied with me prepared me to meet my God, prepared me to experience (*yada'*) him, and prepared me to allow him to know (*yada'*) me! I am so glad they helped me dig deeply into what sin[74] I had, so I could really experience his character of forgiveness, grace, and love. As Jesus said, "He who has been forgiven little loves little" (Luke 7:47). The more we admit our sin, the more we will be able to love God, and know him, and God know us. I am so glad people helped me to come to a place of brokenness over my sin. God's love became very real when that happened as I experienced his offer of grace in an incredible way. I am so glad that people helped me to understand that experiencing God involves listening to him through the reading of his word and that God experiencing me involves me praying and crying out to him.

For good reason, David was a man after God's own heart. I can see it in Psalms, where he opens up his heart to God, and God experiences what is in his heart. I am grateful that my leaders were hard on sin. They were protecting my *yada'* with God. I am thankful

---

74. Most religious groups do not do this and do not prepare people to yada' God, nor him to yada' them.

that many of my disciplers in the past insisted on my obedience to God.[75] They were (whether or not they knew it) helping me with my yada' with God and others. I am so grateful that people who discipled me helped me to learn what total openness is and urged me to express it! Relationships do not exist without it, whether relationships with others or with God.

In John 3:20–21, Jesus states:

> *"Everyone who does evil hates the light and will not come into the light for fear that his deeds will be exposed. But whoever lives by the truth comes into the light, so that it may be seen plainly that what he has done has been done through God."*

Living by the truth means you are open with your life. Your deeds are seen plainly, you are an open book to allow God (and others) to test your character and actions and work through you. Yada' helps make sense of this! Loving the light, loving Jesus, means being open and allowing others and God to experience your character.

It is no wonder Jesus could say in John 8:31–32, "If you hold to my teaching, you are really my disciples. Then you will know (*ginosko*) the truth, and the truth will set you free." It is experiential knowledge that is spoken of here. Truth is to be experienced. Jesus is the truth, and Jesus is to be experienced. Experiencing this truth will set one free. Holding to Jesus' teachings is the first step. It is a way of loving him! It is a way of having an interpersonal experiential relationship with God. Holding to his teachings makes you his disciple, and this actively engages you in yada'.

Yada' helps me understand that loving God means obeying him. He indeed knows (*yada'*) us relationally when he is loved. He experiences our character when we love him. 1 John 5:3 states, "This is love for God: to obey his commands." Love is connected with actions and heart and one's being. Mark 12:28–31 states:

---

75. I admit the way it was done was not always correct or for the right reasons, as one tended to obey just because someone said to and not because it came from the heart, nor was there always an understanding of experiential/relational knowing God. I do believe, however, that many began their Christian walk with yada' but gradually gave it up for serving and following people. I believe and pray that they can reestablish their yada', and if we can now look to the future through the concept of yada' and urge people to obey God as a way of knowing him and being known by him, we will save many from death and cover over a multitude of sins (James 5:20).

One of the teachers of the law came and heard them debating. Noticing that Jesus had given them a good answer, he asked him, "Of all the commandments, which is the most important?"

"The most important one," answered Jesus, "is this: `Hear, O Israel, the Lord our God, the Lord is one. Love the Lord your God with all your heart and with all your soul and with all your mind and with all your strength.' The second is this: `Love your neighbor as yourself.' There is no commandment greater than these."

The love God wants is not intellectual assent, but love that comes from all your heart, all your soul (person), all your mind, and all your strength. In other words, the love God wants to experience from us involves our whole being (including our body and its actions). To love someone else will also mean that your heart, mind, soul, and body are involved, just as when a person loves himself. Loving someone is the act of allowing them to know you. Receiving love from them is an act of you experiencing or knowing them.

Are you engaged in *yada*? Is God knowing you? Are you knowing God? What will God say to you on that judgment day? Will he say, "I never knew you" or "I don't know you" or will he say, "Well done, good and faithful servant!... Come and share your master's happiness!" Are you letting God experience the real you? Are you allowing yourself to experience the real God?

Brothers and sisters, this is, I believe, the greatest blessing I experienced as a result of those in our movement who discipled me and studied with me. It helped me to know God and let God know me. It helped me to become a true disciple, a true son of God. It helped God to become my true Father. I owe them my life. I owe God my life. I hope you have also experienced this blessing, this salvation. Let us never give up *yada*!

CPSIA information can be obtained
at www.ICGtesting.com
Printed in the USA
JSHW020805110423
40171JS00003B/217

9 781953 623867